Praise for *Reverberation*

God uses his all-sufficient Word to grow Christians and gather churches. In this book, Jonathan Leeman presents a glorious vision of this work. His presentation is biblical and theological *as well as* practical and compelling. It's theology applied. He draws the lines *and* colors in the picture. The Bible and life in the local church should reenforce one another in connecting us with God. Is that your experience? As a careful student of the Bible, Jonathan masterfully illustrates what this should look like.

> —Mark Dever, senior pastor
> Capitol Hill Baptist Church, Washington D.C.

Jonathan Leeman has written a very helpful book that examines the role of the Word in the life of the church. So much emphasis has been placed in recent years on the mechanics of preaching, in terms of exegesis, exposition, etc; yet, to preach—and to listen—properly, one must also have an understanding of the theology of preaching, of the Word in action. This book plugs precisely that gap and should be read by pastors, elders, and, indeed, church members.

> —Carl R. Trueman, vice president for Academic Affairs
> Westminster Theological Seminary, PA

Jonathan's book is profound in both its insight and its simplicity. The logic is clear and easy to follow, the conclusions fresh and challenging. Most helpful to me was the refreshing first person honesty woven throughout the book. It is obvious this book is the work of someone who has wrestled with the role of the Word in his life and ministry and become convinced that there is no substitute for it.

> —J.D. Greear, lead pastor,
> The Summit Church

What exactly do we trust the Bible to do? In *Reverberation*, Jonathan Leeman demonstrates what it means to find confidence and security in the sufficiency of the Bible as the Word of God. In this book, we are taken through the life of the church and the life of the Christian into the life of the world in order to understand what it means for Christians to trust the Bible as fully authoritative, fully trustworthy, and absolutely sufficient.

> —Dr. R. Albert Mohler Jr., president
> The Southern Baptist Theological Seminary

Reverberation helps us pastors take a bold stand: Don't be distracted by passing fads. Make the Word of God the centerpiece of your church, pray for power from above, and keep moving forward. Jonathan Leeman's compelling book has stirred my heart. It is now on the agenda of leadership training at our church.
> —Ray Ortlund, lead pastor
> Immanuel Church, Nashville, TN

Fall in love with the Bible once again after reading Jonathan Leeman's *Reverberation*. With a great mixture of conviction, history, and application, *Reverberation* challenges us to place our full attention back on the Scriptures. *Reverberation* is a challenge to return to the power of God's Word being preached and working in the lives of people to create change that then impacts others.
> —Ed Stetzer, president of
> LifeWay Research

I like the way Jonathan Leeman shows how preaching the Word is vital for the church's life and mission—and also that the ministry of the Word can be woven into the entire fabric of the church's life.
> —Mark Galli
> senior managing editor
> *Christianity Today*

I am not sure that we can ever say enough about the authority of God's Word and its incredible power. It is a light, a hammer, a seed, and the list could go on and on, but as we take this Word and not only receive it as instruction, but apply it in our daily walk, what a difference it makes in our world and the world in which we live. Jonathan Leeman has done us a great service in showing the activity of God's Word in us, in the church, and in the world. Read it, and pass it along to your people.
> —Pastor Johnny Hunt
> former president, Southern Baptist Convention

Put this book into the hands of any Christian you wish to give a revolutionizing appreciation of God's Word in the local church. Many believe their lives and their churches are "based on the Bible." But few have as compelling a vision for the word of God reverberating in everything we do as the vision Jonathan Leeman presents here. Leeman is the rare writer who writes with love, clarity, and wisdom about topics that confuse, divide, and frustrate. Here, he writes about the Word of God reverberating through the people of God. The result? A book that makes you love God's Word more, and thereby love the God of the Word more. From page to page, my soul was happy reading this book. *Reverberation* made me thirst for the Word of God!

—Thabiti Anyabwile, senior pastor
First Baptist Church, Grand Cayman

Since Eden, our ancient Foe has never deviated from his primary objective: to overtly and covertly assault God's Word. Satan is ever attempting to hide and distort the power of Scripture and its destiny-determining effect. The Enemy is quite happy for our Bibles to collect cobwebs. In *Reverberation* Jonathan Leeman blows the dust off our Bibles and helpfully guides us to understand, value, and apply the living Word of God. Clearly written, succinct, and deeply thought-provoking, this book will challenge you to give the Bible its rightful primacy in your life.

—Rick Holland, executive pastor
Grace Community Church, Sun Valley, CA

Jonathan Leeman reminds us that the ministry of the Word *begins* in the pulpit, but then it's to reverberate through the songs, prayers, and life of the church. May this book cause us all to hit that reverb button.

—Marshall Shelley
editor, *Leadership journal*

Many churches talk about being "Bible based," but what would a church look like that is really founded on the Scriptures? In this wonderfully written book, Jonathan Leeman shows how the preached Word of the Bible is like a stone dropped into a pool, the ripples of which shape everything about our church life—how we sing, how we pray, how we live, how we disciple each other and how we take the gospel to the world. His section on how the sermon exposes the text of Scripture, announces the gospel, and confronts the sinner is worth the price of the book alone. This is an excellent book. Buy it and be challenged.

—Tony Payne
author of *The Trellis and the Vine*

I love books from authors who love the Word. Jonathan Leeman is one of those authors. In *Reverberation*, Jonathan displays his passion for Scripture, his heart for the church, and his love for King Jesus. This book has deepened my affection for and my confidence in the Word that is powerful unto salvation.

—Trevin Wax, author of
Counterfeit Gospels and *Holy Subversion*

Reverberation is the best succinct reminder I have read of the sufficiency of the Word and Spirit for the life, health, and growth of the church. Amidst myriad methods that have failed to produced sustainable, qualitative growth in congregations, church leaders across denominational lines are looking for what Leeman provides. If they become animated by the biblical principles in this book, their churches will become powerful forces for gospel transformation.

—Matthew Pinson
president, Free Will Baptist Bible College

This book has a vital message. Scripture—and only Scripture—is God's sufficient instrument by which His Spirit gathers the church, changes lives, grows us in Christ, shapes our prayers and praises, and makes disciples. The devil is always trying to replace authentic Christianity with superficial Christianity through de-centering Scripture in the church. With freshness and warmth this clear and readable book commends this crucial truth.

—Christopher Ash, director of the PT Cornhill Training
Course and author of *The Priority of Preaching*

Jonathan Leeman calls the church to fill its tank with the high octane fuel of biblical exposition. He demonstrates how the Word should travel through the body life of the local church. Both pastor and people will be encouraged by *Reverberation.*

—Pastor Ted Traylor
Olive Baptist Church
Pensacola, FL

At a time when every new idea for doing church seems to be both "eye" centered and "I" centered, Jonathan Leeman reminds us that the truly healthy church will always be uniquely aural and uniquely not-about-me. For both reasons, this is a wonderful book.

—John Yates, rector of The Falls Church Anglican

reverberation

jonathan leeman

how God's word brings light, freedom,
and action to His people

MOODY PUBLISHERS

CHICAGO

© 2011 by
JONATHAN LEEMAN

Edited by Jim Vincent
Interior design: Ragont Design
Cover design: Studio Gearbox
Cover image: Getty/Digital Vision

Library of Congress Cataloging-in-Publication Data

Leeman, Jonathan, 1973-
    Reverberation : how God's word brings light, freedom, and action to his people / Jonathan Leeman.
        p. cm.
    Includes bibliographical references and index.
    ISBN 978-0-8024-2299-6 (alk. paper)
    1. Bible—Use. 2. Pastoral theology. I. Title. II. Title: How God's word brings light, freedom, and action to his people.
BS538.3.L44 2010
253—dc22

                                                              2010037134

We hope you enjoy this book from Moody Publishers. Our goal is to provide high-quality, thought-provoking books and products that connect truth to your real needs and challenges. For more information on other books and products written and produced from a biblical perspective, go to www.moodypublishers.com or write to:

Moody Publishers
820 N. LaSalle Boulevard
Chicago, IL 60610

1 3 5 7 9 10 8 6 4 2

Printed in the United States of America

To my parents, Dave and Barbara Leeman,
and my grandmother, Helga Newbould.
You were the first to open God's Word to me.

contents

foreword

The Holy Spirit opened my eyes to the beauty of the gospel of Christ just before my senior year of high school. I have yet to recover.

At the moment He gave me new eyes to see and new ears to hear, He also gave me an insatiable hunger to know more about Him through reading the Scriptures. I began reading other books as well, but I discovered that reading the Bible was different than reading other kinds of literature. It transformed me. It allowed me to see Him. It didn't just give me abstract truth, it gave me Him—the one who has called me out of the "domain of darkness . . . [into] the kingdom of his beloved Son" (Col. 1:13).

In those early days, the God of the universe also

gave me a passion to make sure others know about His grace and mercy for them in the cross of Christ. By the time I graduated there wasn't one friend with whom I had not shared the gospel. Several of them became believers. But others wanted nothing to do with Jesus. They seemed to despise Him without knowing Him. I was painfully learning that the aroma of Christ will smell like death to some, regardless of how it's presented (2 Cor. 2:16). Yet I also knew there was no way around it: To introduce people to a saving knowledge of Christ, you must speak words, and you must speak what are sometimes offensive words.

I have been a pastor and elder for eight years now, and I remain convinced that speaking words—biblical words and gospel words—must be central in churches and in ministry. Don't misunderstand: I believe in contextualization and making sure that the Bible and the truths of God can be understood and applied to contemporary circumstances. It's my strong opinion that everyone contextualizes, whether they're contextualizing to the sixteenth century, the twentieth century, or today. Yet I also understand that we can become more concerned with "reaching people" than with being faithful to the Scriptures. And by neglecting the Scriptures, we lose track of what we are reaching people *to*. If it's *to* a God other than the holy, triune creator God of the Bible, or if it's *to* a savior other than the one in the Scriptures who died to appease God's wrath toward sinful men, justifying completely those who repent and believe, then we're no longer offering salvation at all, and we're not building a "church." We might have gathered a good group of people who do good things, but it's not the bride of Christ.

It's been our experience at The Village Church in Dallas that people will both accept and reject God's Word, in spite of anything else that we might do in our ministry. By being faithful to proclaim the God and Savior of the Scriptures, some lives have been transformed and wooed to God. Others have been offended. You will never be able to make Jesus cool enough for everyone to love and worship Him.

It's not just in the "Bible Belt" of Dallas that churches are experiencing large numbers of people coming to know Christ and surrendering their lives to Jesus through the proclamation of the Word. I can speak of pastor friends in Seattle, Manhattan, Boston, Washington D.C., and other major cities in the United States and abroad whose faithfulness to the God of the Scriptures has yielded deep people who worship passionately, cling to biblical community, and share the beauty of the gospel both locally and internationally.

In *Reverberation*, Jonathan Leeman does a tremendous job of demonstrating why we can have faith in God's Word to create, sustain, and empower daily obedience *to the Word*. He encourages, rebukes, and warns us to keep the Scriptures central so that we might see what God wants to create instead of trying to create ourselves without the authority and power we were meant to wield.

I agree with so many that something is off in evangelicalism. Jonathan has pinned down one of the great errors—a growing loss of confidence in God's Word. So read this book. My prayer is that the Holy Spirit would work powerfully through it to call you to biblical faithfulness in preaching and living.

MATT CHANDLER
Lead Pastor/Teaching Pastor
The Village Church

introduction: one thing is necessary

Like many children who grow up in church, I learned how to endure the blah-blah-blah of long sermons at a young age.

When you're five or six, you survive them by scrutinizing everything within arm's reach: the back of the head in front of you, the misshapen ears, the offering envelopes which you fold into a tiny ball, the half-length pencils whose tips you break. Sometimes you poke your little brother, which provokes your mother and keeps things interesting.

When you're fifteen or sixteen, you can listen to some of the blah-blah-blah, but your attention comes and goes. Maybe you daydream. Maybe you wonder what the other teenagers in the room think of you, especially the members of the opposite sex.

I also remember at this age watching the preacher walk around the platform. He would stroll to one side of the pulpit nonchalantly, as if he were walking up to you at a backyard barbeque. Then he'd amble to the other side of the pulpit, like he wanted to say hello to a family who just arrived. Sometimes he'd casually lean sideways with one hand resting on the pulpit. The whole thing intrigued me. It was so friendly and down to earth.

Of course, I wasn't really listening to what he said. About the only thing I heard were illustrations about Michael Jordan and the Chicago Bulls. It was the 1980s, and the Bulls were on the rise. And we lived in a suburb of Chicago. Mention Jordan's name and everyone would hop to attention.

Yet let's be honest. It's not just the five-year-olds and fifteen-year-olds who struggle to avoid yawning in sermons. It's adults, too. We all phase in and out. Maybe your brain gets stuck in a spin cycle about a conversation from yesterday. Maybe you start planning Sunday afternoon's "to-do" list. To this day, I can catch myself tuning out, especially when the preacher mires down in some biblical lesson. But the moment that he begins telling a story, my ears perk up. Does that happen to you?

All of this causes a person to ask whether preaching is that important to the lives of Christians and churches.

The preaching didn't make much of a difference in my life in high school, or in the lives of some of my friends and their parents. I left high school for college, quit attending church, and jumped into the party scene. So did many of my friends. By God's grace, I came back to Christ and to His church after college. But many of those friends did not. Today they are stuck in agnosticism, materialism, alcoholism, and more. Many of the parents I looked up to are now divorced.

What good did all those sermons do?

Something with More Octane?

It makes you wonder: Isn't there something with a little more octane for powering life and growth in our churches than a guy standing up front talking?

My guess is that many Christians today want sermons and songs that are true and broadly biblical, yet for many of us, rightly or wrongly, a strong ministry of the Word is not a top priority. When we first walk into a church, our attention fixes on other things, like the style of the music, the availability of good children's programming, or even the look and feel of the room. Honestly, we can evaluate churches like people evaluate trendy urban restaurants—"how's the ambiance?"

Meanwhile, church leaders, to the extent that they oblige our interest in other things, seem to have lost confidence in the ministry of the Word. Sure enough, the answers you'll find in books and conferences for church leaders have them looking every which way. They're told they need better lay visitation, more dynamic worship, holistic small groups, more participatory decision making, better personal accessibility, adequate parking, solid financial resources, attractive programs, the presence of the Holy Spirit, passionate spirituality, gift-oriented ministry, speaking in tongues, visionary leadership, strategic leadership, empowered leadership, loving relationships, contemporary worship, God-exalting worship, high-impact worship, creative worship forms, liturgical reverence, a vibrant public witness, incarnational ministries, missional living, contextualized outreach, a sophisticated knowledge of culture . . . and the list goes on.

Are any of these things bad? Not at all. Most are fine or even good. The question is, Where are we placing our confidence? As Christians, we believe God created the universe by His Word. We've heard about Ezekiel bringing dead bones to life with words. And we know Paul commanded Timothy to "Preach the word." Yes, yes, we know all that. But . . .

Let's be realistic. Our day is a day that's captivated by images. It's an age for the eye, not the ear. "Give us flat screens and big screens," the people say. "Give us satellite feeds and video-on-demand." It's how our brains are wired. My oldest daughter learned the alphabet when she was three from a family of frogs by watching a video called "The Letter Factory." I didn't mean for this to happen. But I hit "play," and it happened. What can I say? She's now been conditioned by video. It's how she learns.

Church leaders are catching on. I remember learning about "faith" in one devotion by watching a movie clip with Harrison Ford, where he steps off a cliff and onto an invisible bridge to save his dad's life. I can still remember the picture.

God's Word, working through God's Spirit, is God's primary instrument for growing God's church.

Of course it's not just video clips that people want to see. They want to see good deeds in action. People today are enamored with authenticity, which means *being* something, not *saying* something. I can't tell you how many times I've heard a young Christian repeat those words attributed to St. Francis, "Preach the gospel at all times; when necessary, use words."

Surely images have more octane than words. A picture's worth a thousand words, we say. And seeing is believing. Haven't you ever found yourself midway through a movie, and sympathetic with the main characters, only to realize that you don't know their names? But you certainly know their faces.

The Most Powerful Force in the Universe

How important, really, is preaching the Bible to the life and existence of local churches? Not important? Kind of important? One of several things that are important?

My guess is that, if you're a Christian, you pay at least lip service to the idea that God's Word is important. Yet my first goal in this book is to help you see theologically and practically how uniquely essential it is. I want to help you see that God's Word, working through God's Spirit, is God's primary instrument for growing God's church. In fact, God's Word is the most powerful force in the universe. God created the universe through His Word (Gen. 1:3). He is recreating it through His Word (2 Cor. 4:6). And He sustains all things by His Word (Heb. 1:3).

God speaking involves all three persons, as the Father speaks through the Son by the Spirit. All three wonderfully conspire to pour forth their power through speech, to accomplish their single will through words.

What's more, God creates and grows His church through His Word, which is the second goal of this book. God grows us as individuals and as local churches through our ears.

Then again, maybe you "know" all that. If so, it's worth asking whether that confidence translates into how you choose a church, or how you try to lead, structure, and grow your church if you're a church leader.

Let me put it like this. Picture in your mind some church you have known. Now, for just a moment, take away the programs. Take away the children's nursery. Take away the parking lot and the musical instruments and the bulletins. Take away the building. Take away everything but the people of the church itself. Imagine all these members of the church standing together in a field. If you like, you can imagine it's a sunny day and that nobody's getting wet. Make the field as nice and flowery as you like. The point is, all you have are the people.

Once you have this church in your head, ask the question: What do we *need* to grow this church in both numbers and spiritual depth? Do we need the building back? Or the musical instruments or bulletins? What must we have?

Surely we need some water for baptizing people. And somebody needs to bring the bread and cup for the Lord's Supper. Both of these things are necessary for constituting the church as a church. Some people might also say that particular ministerial offices are necessary for constituting the church as a church, but let's leave that question aside for the moment. What's absolutely necessary for life and growth?

Answer: God's Word working through God's Spirit. Somebody has to pick up a Bible and read it. And someone has to explain it so that people will understand it. When this happens, the Spirit begins to work upon people's hearts, causing them to believe the words and give a proper weight to them. The people then repeat the words in their songs and prayers. They discover, most remarkably, that they can speak to God as guided by these biblical words. They also repeat the words of God to one another throughout the week. They help each other discern His will for their lives. Then their lives begin to be shaped by the words, so that they begin to live differently at work and at home. They discover that these words are life-giving, hope-giving, and love-producing.

So they run and call others who have not yet heard these words to hear them. Words produce actions, and then those actions and words work together to give witness to the power of God to salvation, a salvation that begins now and stretches into eternity.

Leaving aside, as I say, the issues of baptism, the Lord's

Supper, and ministerial office, what do we see in this picture of these people standing in our imaginary field? We see the church forming and coming to life. We see it growing. I'm not saying that any of the things that we removed from the picture are bad, and that we should not use them. I assume that church buildings, musical instruments, nurseries, and maybe even a few programs are good gifts from the Lord. God can and does use microphones, charismatic leaders, bulletins, a pleasant ambiance, and sometimes, perhaps, denominational structures. The point is, none of these things is necessary, because none of these things is the source of a church's life and growth. They're all extraneous or instrumental, and we cannot let them jump to the top of the priority list.

What about obedient lives—aren't they necessary? Surely, but the key is to recognize that God has a different role for words and actions. Words create; actions are the creation. You see the same division of labor in Genesis 1 between words and physical matter. Words created; the physical universe was the creation. Now, apply that division of labor to the spiritual universe: spiritual words create spiritual actions.

True spiritual life is produced in the heart only when the Father speaks with creation power through the Son and by the Spirit. I'm not talking about reading magic incantations. I'm talking about the power of God for giving light to the mind, affections to the heart, and freedom to the will, which then move hands and feet into holy action.

Surprisingly, even lives of love and holiness are finally inadequate for knowing God apart from the spoken word, since words are necessary for "translating" or "interpreting" such love and holiness. People can talk about the "transformative power" of love, but apart from words about God, all such transformation is finally secular or godless. If you act kindly toward me, I'm going to praise you, not God. My opinion of God will not change one bit. You must *say* to me, "Don't thank me. Thank God who is kind and teaches me to be kind." Our invisible God is only known through His Word.

The same is true of baptism or the Lord's Supper. Unless these pictures or symbols are explained, a person cannot know what they *mean*. Words must accompany them in order to give them meaning.

One Thing Is Necessary

"One thing is necessary," Jesus said to Martha as she bustled away serving the party, unlike Mary "who sat at the Lord's feet and listened to his teaching" (Luke 10:39, 41). Jesus' rebuke of Martha catches us off guard, because it seems obvious that acts of service are better than words. Actions speak louder than words, we say. And talk is cheap. Yes, but Christianity begins not with what we do, but with the announcement of what God has done. Furthermore, it's only words that can challenge our self-rule. Melodies or visual images can inspire us, encourage us, or cause us to grieve. But only words can command us to surrender control of our lives and yield them to Christ. We'll discuss this idea further in subsequent chapters.

One thing is necessary in our churches—hearing God's Word through preaching, reading, singing, and praying.

What about the power of sight? What about the fact that people today have been conditioned by an image-driven marketplace?

There's nothing new here. People have always been driven by sight. The Israelites felt fear at the sight of Goliath. The lover feels attraction at the sight of his beloved in the Song of Solomon. The temple was decorated with bronze pomegranates and gold flowers. And the apostle John warns his readers about "the desires of the eyes" (1 John 2:16). Sight moves people. It draws them and repulses them. That's how God created us.

At the same time, we live in the "age of the ear," as my friend Mark Dever calls it, an age that extends from Adam and Eve's eviction from the garden of Eden to Christ's final return. After Adam and Eve sinned in the garden, God withdrew Himself from the sight of all humanity. He forbade His people from making any representation of Him. And He permitted His favored prophet, Moses, only to see His back. Christ did appear among men, but even here the only physical description we get comes from one Old Testament prophet's characterization of what Jesus *didn't* look like: He had no majesty or beauty that we should desire to look at Him (Isa. 53:2). The Gospels themselves give us nothing of what Jesus looked like. Apparently the Bible doesn't want us to focus on the sight of Jesus.

One day, of course, this will all change. The Lord Himself will descend from heaven, His people will be caught up with Him, and we will "see him as he is" (1 John 3:2; 1 Thess. 4:16). Yet until that day, we cannot see God, we can only hear from Him, His prophets, and His apostles. We come to know him not through sight but through sound, the sound of His Word read and taught.

I'm glad that we Christians affirm the authority of God's Word in our theology books. But now we need to fight for faith in His Word, particularly in how we approach what's central in our churches. Church leaders need to fight for faith in His Word. Christians need to fight for such faith. It's all too easy to put our faith in the things which more visibly and immediately draw people.

Reverberation

At the same time, a loss of confidence in God's Word is not the only error to avoid. If we shift our gaze to the more doctrinally selective churches, particularly of the Reformed variety, we will hear strong affirmations of the "ministry of the Word" and "building the church on the Word." And typically these phrases refer to the teaching ministry of the Sunday morning pulpit. The problem here, however, is that God's Word is not always massaged throughout the life of the congregation, like yeast through dough. People show up on Sunday for the sermon, and often do little more. The ministry of the Word stops at noon.

The hearts of people both absorb and project the sounds of His effectual Word.

This book, however, hopes to illustrate that the "ministry of the Word" indeed *begins* in the pulpit, but then it must *continue* through the life of the church as members echo God's Word back and forth to one another. The word reverberates, as in an echo chamber. In a real echo chamber, sound reverberates off walls. In the church, it's the hearts of people that both absorb and project the sounds of His effectual Word.

Putting it like this first occurred to me when Tim Lane, director of the Christian Counseling and Education Foundation, was talking about the "ministry of the Word" in an interview I did with him for the *9Marks eJournal*. Tim said this:

The ministry of the Word doesn't stop [with the preaching]; it continues throughout the church. The discipling ministry, the children's ministry, the youth ministry, the missions work, the worship ministry, the friendships and families—all of this operates on the same page by being Word oriented and Christ centered. Elders and deacons are taking the Word into their work. Parents are learning to bring the gospel into how they train their kids. Husbands and wives are thinking about the centrality of the gospel as they relate to one another. And the list goes on and on.

Hearing Tim's words, I couldn't help but think of reverberating words.

Picture it this way. The evangelist or the preacher opens his mouth and utters a word, God's Word. But the Word doesn't sound just once. It echoes or reverberates. It reverberates through the church's music and prayers. It reverberates through the conversations between elders and members, members and guests, older Christians and younger ones. God's words bounce around the life of the church, like the metal ball in a pinball machine.

But the reverberating words shouldn't stop there. The church building doors should open and God's words should echo out the doors, down the street, and into the members' homes and workplaces. The reverberations of sound that began in the pulpit should eventually be bouncing off the walls in dining rooms, kitchens, and children's bedrooms; off gymnasium walls, cubicle dividers, and the insides of city bus windows; through e-mails, text messages, and Internet pages.

The goal of this book is to follow this path. We are going to take a theological and practical look at how God's Word establishes the church and grows it. The Word grows the church as unbelievers are saved and baptized into it, and then it grows church members in their life together. My hope for church leaders reading this book is that they will grow in their conviction of what they must *do* to build a church. And my hope for all Christians reading it is that they will grow in their conviction of what they *need* and therefore *require* in their churches.

Nothing New Here

Many of the books being published about the local church these days are looking for something new—some new way to engage with the culture, some new way to structure our churches, some new way to appeal to outsiders. And surely there is a place for such conversations. But I'd propose that churches become healthy and Christians become vibrant through the same things today as they did in New Testament churches: through evangelizing, preaching, teaching, singing, praying, and discipling one another with God's Word. True life, kingdom life, exciting life, will be created in our churches through nothing new, but through something quite old.

My plan, therefore, is to point to stuff that is really old, really good, and really powerful. I begin in chapter 1 by introducing the topic with the evangelist, who is the first to speak God's words of life-giving power. It might have made better sense to begin the book with a theological foundation of the Word, but I've held that off until chapter 2, because I want to start with real-life pictures of the Word in action before asking what's happening behind the scenes.

With that foundation in place, the rest of the book follows the path of the reverberating Word. Chapter 3 traces it into the individual's heart. Chapter 4 watches it gather the local church. Chapters 5 to 7 listen to its reverberations in the sermon. Chapters 8 to 10 follow the Word through music, prayer, and discipleship. Finally, we'll cycle back to evangelism once more as we consider the church's mission and its purposes in scattering.

As we trace this single theme, like a needle and thread through the different patches of the church's life, my prayer is that Christians and church leaders from every polity will be strengthened in faith in the sufficiency of God's Word.

PART 1
the word

1 } the word invites and divides

Richard Elelu had no interest in actually reading the Bible. He was a Muslim, after all, and he lived in one of the strongest Muslim enclaves in Nigeria. Still, he did figure out one way to put the Bible given to him by a Christian to good use: its crackly thin pages were perfect for rolling joints and cigarettes.

"Papers for rolling our own cigarettes were expensive," Richard said. "So we would tear out pages from the Bibles and use them for our rolling papers."

On one occasion in 1978, Richard tore a page from the Bible for rolling a joint, but ended up stuffing it into his pocket. That night, bored and unable to sleep, he pulled the page of the Bible from his pocket and read these words from Psalm 34:8: "O, taste and see that the

Lord is good; how happy is the man who takes refuge in Him" (NASB). For the next three weeks he could not get the verse out of his head. He returned to the Christian who had shared the gospel with him. One night, alone in his room, Richard prayed, "Lord God, I want to taste You like this verse says," and that same evening accepted Christ as Savior and Lord.

Richard's Muslim family and community did not respond very well. At first they expressed concern. Then they displayed anger. And then he received death threats. Richard was the first convert in the community, and so it felt like a grave threat to everyone. Local mosque leaders denounced him on the mosque's outdoor loudspeakers. His own father told him that he would rather see him dead. He had to spend every night at a different missionary's house because of the danger.

Richard left for another community in Nigeria to attend Bible school. Once that was completed, he returned to his home community to pastor a church of factory and government workers who had migrated there. The death threats then resumed at a rapid clip, as well as acts of vandalism against his church building. The police looked the other way. Richard eventually moved to the United States to protect his wife and children and to gain more Bible training. I didn't know him at the time, but Richard and I were seminary classmates.[1]

It all started with a Bible verse on a wadded up piece of paper dug out of a pocket.

History's Great Dividing Line

There are a number of biblical ways to describe the change that occurred in Richard's life. We could say he moved

- from non-Christian to Christian,
- from unbelief to belief,
- from being a lover of the world to a lover of God, or

• from belonging to the kingdom of Satan to the kingdom of God.

But here's one more way to describe this change, and it's a change as dramatic as any of these others: Richard moved *from being someone who rejected God's Word to someone who listened to it.*

In a true Christian, all these changes work together. The person who truly loves God also trusts God, submits to God's kingdom rule, and listens to His Word.

That's not to say these different things *must* go together. Someone can believe that God exists, like the demons do, and yet not love God (James 2:19). And someone can listen to God's Word, or at least appear to, like the Pharisees who "search the Scriptures," and yet not really submit to God (John 5:39).

In spite of all that, it remains the case that a Christian, by definition, is someone who listens to God's Word because he or she loves God. And a non-Christian is someone who, regardless of appearances, does not truly listen to God's Word because that person does not love God.

This is the dividing line that runs through all history and humanity: God's people listen to God's Word; no one else does. Every human belongs to one category or the other. There is no third category. Trace the storyline of the whole Bible and you'll see that this is one of its main lessons. They are:

• *God sets the stage, but man rebels (Genesis 1–3):* God created Adam to image God's own rule over creation. This meant submitting to God's words, represented by just one command. Adam and Eve didn't listen, and God condemned both for listening to someone else's voice (Gen. 1:26–28; 2:16–17; 3:17).

- *God promises salvation (Genesis 4–50):* God still intended to use a people for His creation purposes— bringing His blessing and rule to the earth. God soon called Abraham, and Abraham believed God and followed. God's people in Genesis are those who believe God's Word and are willing to live or die by it, even if they have nothing else (Gen. 12:1–3; 15:6; Rom. 4:5; Heb. 11:4–22; James 2:23).

- *God calls His people to obedience (Exodus to Deuteronomy):* God said He would use Abraham's children as "a kingdom of priests and a holy nation" in order to present a picture of God's character and loving rule to all the nations, but only if they "obey my voice and keep my covenant." God reveals both His love and law through words, which He asked Israel to keep: "And these words that I command you today shall be on your heart. You shall teach them . . . and shall talk of them. . . . You shall bind them . . . and they shall be as frontlets between your eyes. You shall write them . . ." The Pentateuch's primary lesson seems to be, "Hear, O Israel" (Deut. 4:5–8; 6:4, 6–9; cf. Ex. 19:5–6; Deut. 28:1–2, 15).

- *God describes the blessed and wise life (the OT Wisdom Literature):* Two kinds of people are presented at the start of the Psalms: the blessed man who delights in God's law and becomes as fruitful as Eden, and the wicked man who rejects God's law and is blown away like chaff. The Psalms as a whole then picture how the ideal man turns to God and His Word through all of life's circumstances. Proverbs, too, presents two types of people: the wise son who fears the Lord and obeys his father's words, and the fool who rejects them (Psalm 1).

- *God declares the ugly, disobedient reality of human nature (the OT Histories):* The picture of an ideal God-listening, God-imaging people was shattered like a mirror into countless pieces by the actual history of Israel. God rejected them because "they would not listen . . . rejected his decrees and the covenant . . . followed worthless idols . . . imitated the nations around them . . . did the things the Lord had forbidden them to do . . . [and] forsook all the commandments." Keep in mind, this ancient nation is a picture of all of us—a parable of humanity (2 Kings 17:14–16 NIV; Rom. 8:7).

- *God promises to create a God-listening, God-imaging people by His Spirit (the OT Prophets):* In addition to reporting bad news, the prophets offered good news: God would cleanse His people of sin, and enable them to keep His words: "I will sprinkle clean water on you, and you shall be clean from all your uncleannesses . . . I will put my Spirit within you, and cause you to walk in my statutes and be careful to obey my rules" (Ezek. 36:25, 27; cf. Deut. 30:6–8; Jer. 31:31–34).

- *The Word—Christ incarnate—comes, obeys, and makes commands (the Gospels):* God's Word became flesh, obeyed the Father completely, and called a new people to abide in God's love by keeping His words. Jesus Himself lived on "every word that comes from the mouth of God," and then concluded His earthly ministry by telling His disciples to make more disciples, "teaching them to observe all I have commanded you" (Matt. 4:4; 28:20; cf. John 1:14; 5:19; 15:10).

- *God's new covenant people gather to hear God's Word (Acts):* God's new covenant people, who receive the promised Holy Spirit, gather primarily to hear words from God and then to speak words back to Him in prayer: "And they devoted themselves to the apostles' teaching and the fellowship, to the breaking of bread and the prayers." This is what church leaders should devote themselves to entirely: "But we will devote ourselves to prayer and to the ministry of the word" (Acts 2:42; 6:4).

- *God's new covenant people gather to dwell in God's Word (the Epistles):* "Let the word of Christ dwell in you richly, teaching and admonishing one another in all wisdom, singing psalms and hymns and spiritual songs" (Col. 3:16). The epistles, which look back on Christ's life and interpret it, help God's people to dwell in the Word of Christ and grow in God's love: "If anyone obeys his word, God's love is truly made complete in him" (1 John 2:5 NIV).

- *God's new covenant people will persevere in God's Word to the end (Revelation):* Jesus equates keeping His Word and proclaiming His name. He said to one church, "I know that you have little strength, yet you have kept my word and have not denied my name" (Rev. 3:8 NIV).

One of the main lessons of the Bible is that there are two ways to live: We can listen to God's Word or we can reject it. A man cannot serve two masters, said Jesus. Therefore, when He proclaimed His kingdom, He called all people to repent and believe. He was drawing a line in the sand: His rule or ours. God's Word or our own. It's one or the other. There is no in between. And Jesus will identify Himself with those who listen to God's Word, even more than with his family and nation: "My mother and my brothers are those who hear the word of God and do it" (Luke 8:21).

Now, God's people are not justified by their ability to keep God's Word, nor will they keep it perfectly. But God's Spirit changes their basic heart posture toward God's Word, so they fight to listen and obey, even if imperfectly. Their hearts become like the lover's, who eagerly anticipates a note from his beloved. Or the soldier's, who is surrounded by enemy fire and straining his ears for words of coming help. God's people want to hear from God, even if indwelling sin continues to fight against this new desire. Let me sum up all of this in four points:

- *God created Adam, you, and me to image Himself.*
- *To image God, we must listen to God.*
- *God's people, by definition, are those who listen.* That's exactly what Jesus says: "My sheep hear my voice, and I know them, and they follow me." Those who are not his sheep don't listen: "I told you, and you do not believe. . . .You do not believe because you are not part of my flock" (John 10:27, 25–26).
- *God's Word, therefore, divides.* It divides the Christian from the non-Christian. It divides the Christian in half, separating the "old man" and the "new man."

As the author of the Hebrews puts it, "For the word of God is living and active, sharper than any two-edged sword, piercing to the division of soul and of spirit, of joints and of marrow, and discerning the thoughts and intentions of the heart" (Heb. 4:12).

The Temptation to Soften

If the Word of God divides, it's not hard to guess which temptations will lurk before Christians. First, we will be tempted to unite people around something other than God's divisive Word, like music, or style, or acts of service. We'll consider this in chapter 3. Second, we'll be tempted to water down God's Word. To soften it. Bringing up the Bible can be like walking into a room waving a sword. People are going to fight or flee! So keep it in the scabbard, right?

Of course not. When we do, we invite people to something Jesus is not inviting them to, like inviting friends to a basketball game when Jesus *means* to invite them to a wedding. Jesus has specifically invited people to a wedding, *knowing that many will refuse to put on wedding garments* (see Matt. 22:11–13). Believe it or not, Jesus *means* to divide people through His call to repentance (Matt. 10:34f). When we soften the invitation, leaving out the tough bits, we oppose His very purposes.

> *Jesus* means to *divide people* through His call to repentance.

Furthermore, Jesus' words work. They accomplish their purposes. His sheep listen, as we just saw (John 10:16, 27). Those who don't belong to His flock don't listen (v. 26). When we as Jesus followers call out with His voice, people will accept us or reject us depending on whether or not they are His. This is how the apostle John puts it in one of his letters: "Whoever knows God listens to us; whoever is not from God does not listen to us" (1 John 4:6).

What does this mean in practical terms? It means the life of the church must begin with something very simple and basic: an invitation.

The Invitation

Richard had to be invited. For him the invitation started with a torn and wrinkled piece of paper with words written by a man three thousand years ago. "Taste and see the Lord is good."

For my fellow elder Matt, the invitation came from an open-air preacher on his college campus. Many Christians today may cringe at the idea of a street-side, soapbox preacher, and for two years of college Matt mocked him as well. Then, in a third year, Matt listened, repented, and believed. Today, the Word reverberates through Matt as an elder as well as director of a Christian ministry to other churches.

For my fellow church member Israel, the invitation came from a stranger on the street when he was stationed with the army in South Korea. A guy walked up to him and started talking about Jesus. That's not a popular evangelistic strategy these days either. But Israel eventually attended this man's church, repented, and believed. Today the Word reverberates through Israel as he performs Christian hip-hop. He's produced several albums.

For my friend Claudia, who works as a magazine editor in Washington, D.C., the invitation came from a middle-aged Southern Baptist pastor named Mark who wears suits and ties on Sunday, hardly the hip picture you would find on the cover of *Relevant* magazine. Mark led Claudia through a series of Bible studies in the Gospel of Mark, and she repented and believed. Today you can see evidence for the reverberations of God's Word through Claudia in Bill. Bill thought he was a Christian because he had been raised in church. But shortly after her conversion Claudia told him what some say you should never say: "You're not a Christian." She invited him to repent and believe, which he did. Today Bill and Claudia are married and both are members of our church.

How do you build a church from scratch? Through the evangelist. The evangelist might be a page of the Bible, a zealous Christian on the street, or a tie-wearing pastor. But someone must share the *evangel*, the good news of Jesus Christ. Someone must speak words. And these words must do four things:

- explain how good and holy God is;
- explain the predicament of our corruption and guilt and God's just wrath;
- tell about the king who came to reintroduce His life-giving rule in the lives of a new people by living and dying for their sake, bearing the penalty for their sin, and then conquering death through His resurrection; and
- invite them to confess that Jesus is this Lord and King, to trust entirely in His finished work on the cross, and to follow Him.

The beginning of John Bunyan's great book *The Pilgrim's Progress* gets it just right. The main character named Christian happens upon a book that warns him of his impending death and judgment, which reduces him to tears and panic. His family scoffs at him, unable to understand his consternation. Then the character Evangelist appears and tells him, "Fly from the wrath to come." A little later he tells him, "The just shall live by faith." And he reminds him of the Lord's words, "Strive to enter in at the straight gate."

This is where the life of the church begins—with the evangelist. The evangelist proclaims the good news and invites people to receive it.

How Beautiful the Feet!

I admit it; evangelism is hard. Not too long ago, I was on a game preserve in Africa, sitting in the front seat of a Land Rover next to the driver for several hours. In between the driver's explanation of the differences between rhino and giraffe digestive processes, I was asking myself how I could possibly turn the conversation to the gospel. At one point I started to, but he interrupted, "There's a chameleon!" He slammed on the brakes. We piled out of the car and looked at the lizard. We piled back in. And I began wondering once more how I could get back to the topic. Bottom line: I didn't. Why not? There are probably a number of reasons: fear of man, wrong priorities, underestimating how important it is.

Another reason I didn't share the gospel is because I forgot what the Bible says about evangelists. It says they have beautiful feet! Listen to this: "How beautiful on the mountains are the feet of those who bring good news, who proclaim peace, who bring good tidings, who proclaim salvation, who say to Zion, 'Your God reigns!' " (Isa. 52:7 NIV).

You can almost imagine standing on the streets of a city living under the threat of war, looking up at nearby mountains, and seeing a lone runner descending toward the city shouting, "Peace! Salvation!" How beautiful are those feet! The word for "beautiful" is the same word used in the Song of Solomon to describe the beauty of the beloved, her cheeks, her face, her mouth. These things are good to behold.

Paul presents the same emphasis on the messenger in Romans 10 when he quotes this verse from Isaiah. He writes, "How are they to believe in him of whom they have never heard? And how are they to hear without someone preaching? And how are they to preach unless they are sent? As it is written, 'How beautiful are the feet of those who preach the good news!'" (vv. 14–15). Paul knows that "faith comes from hearing" (v. 17).

Why is this messenger so beautiful? So delight-provoking in the heart? Here are five reasons:

1. *The messenger, the preacher, the evangelist, Isaiah 52 tells us, brings news.* He doesn't bring a list of things that must be done, or an argument. No, he announces what God has done. The job is completed. The war is won. Head on home, folks. Christ has paid the penalty.

2. *The messenger is beautiful because he pronounces peace.* Most people don't think of themselves as at war with God and their fellow human beings. But apart from Christ we are. By nature we put ourselves first, which means we're living in a permanent state of strife with God and others. Then, into the middle of that strife, a messenger comes with an offer of peace with God and God's people. Christ bound up the forces of evil. He paid this penalty for sin. He brings *shalom*—which is not just an absence of conflict, but harmony, accord, wholeness, unity. How beautiful is the person who rides into town proclaiming "Peace!"

> God's rule is peace-giving, life-giving, and beauty-creating.

3. *The messenger is beautiful because the tidings he brings are good.* It's so good. If you're a Christian, you have experienced the goodness of forgiveness. The goodness of knowing God's favor. The goodness of freedom from sin's enslavement. The goodness of transformation. The goodness of fellowship grounded in the gospel. The goodness of faith, hope, and love. Don't we now want our friends and family, our neighbors and enemies, to know this same goodness?

4. *The messenger is beautiful because he proclaims salvation.* What do people need to be saved from? Poverty? Empty stomachs? HIV/AIDs? War and strife? Death? Yes, all of that. But all of these are consequences of the real problem: our sin against God and God's wrath against us. In fact, God means for the gut-wrenching sight of poverty, sickness, and death to serve as loving warnings of an

even greater judgment to come. How beautiful are the feet of the one who comes and says, "Salvation—this way."

5. *The messenger is beautiful because he comes to pronounce the reign of God.* And God's rule is gentle and light. It's peace-giving, life-giving, and beauty-creating. Our non-Christian friends, meanwhile, live in bondage to the oppressive rule of sinful desire, worldly ideologies, and fallen spiritual powers. How beautiful is the evangelist who pronounces the freedom of God's rule!

How beautiful are the people who shared the gospel with Richard Elelu, and my fellow elder Matt, and Israel, and Claudia!

How beautiful are the people who shared the gospel with your favorite historical Christians, and your favorite church leaders, and your favorite Christian authors, and your dear Christian friends! What if, out of fear or busy schedules, no one had ever said the words "Jesus" or "sin" or "cross" or "repent" to any of these people?

What if no one ever shared the gospel with you? Not a single word of it. Nothing. Unless you believe in a different gospel than I do, wouldn't you have to say there would be no forgiveness of sin for you? No escape from sin's grip? No knowledge of God's love in Christ? How beautiful is the person who shared the gospel with you!

The Question on the Plane

The first man onto the airplane was old and needed special assistance. He took a seat in the first row by the window. I was the second person onto the plane and took the aisle seat in his row. Right away, we began talking, and he told me that he wondered if this would be his last flight since he was so old. The thought hit me: "What if no one has shared the gospel with him? He's about to meet his Judge in a perilous state." So in a soft and pastoral tone I responded, "Should it be your last trip, would you say that you're ready to meet God?"

He was hard of hearing, and asked me to repeat the question. I became conscious of the flight attendants who were hovering four feet away, as well as every single embarking passenger walking by close enough to brush my leg. Still, I figured I could raise my voice a little bit and not be a distraction: "Would you say that you're ready to meet God?" I repeated. He replied, once more, "What did you say?"

At this point, it occurred to me that the words "Are you ready to meet God" might cause some dismay among airplane passengers in these post-September 11 days. Still, I couldn't think of anything else to say, and I was determined not to let fear of man stop me. This could be an eternity-determining question for him. So basically I shouted, "WOULD YOU SAY YOU'RE READY TO MEET GOD?!" Yes, at that point, any "pastoral" in my "pastoral tone" was surely gone.

Gratefully, the flight crew didn't call security and escort me off the plane. I did have a good conversation with the man. I hope a seed was planted and he has since repented and believed. God knows.

I am fairly positive that I am not a good evangelist. But I try to be faithful, which is the main thing that Christ asks of all of us to be. After all, *He* is the one who will give the growth!

It's the growth that God gives that we turn to in the next chapter. It turns out that inviting people with God's Word is far more powerful than I've let on so far.

Note

1. What an honor! Most of the details of this story can be found in Victoria Moon, "Nigerian Lost Family, Risked Death, But Gained a Savior," *The Western Recorder*, weekly paper of the Kentucky Baptist Convention (November 5, 2002): p. 9. I spoke with Richard by phone to confirm this story and gain his permission to use it.

Recommended Reading

Dever, Mark. *Gospel and Personal Evangelism*. Wheaton, Ill.: Crossway, 2007.

Stiles, Mark. *Marks of a Messenger*. Downers Grove, Ill.: InterVarsity, 2010.

Packer, J. I. *Evangelism and the Sovereignty of God*. Downers Grove, Ill.: InterVarsity, 1991. First published in 1961.

2 } the word acts

"Words, words, words."

Have you heard that phrase? It's from Shake-speare's play *Hamlet*. Another character asks Prince Hamlet what book he is reading, to which he replies, "Words, words, words." It's a despondent response. Surely the book was saying *something*, but the hopeless Hamlet found that *something* to be meaningless. The words were no more than syllables of sound. Splashes of ink on paper.

Shakespeare wrote *Hamlet* around 1600, but here was a postmodern moment if there ever was one. It's awfully tempting these days to agree with Hamlet about the emptiness of words. There's no real mean-ing; there are just words. There's no real truth; there are just words. We believe in words like we trust in promises—very little. Both words and promises are unstable. Sometimes they will be kept but most of the time they'll be broken. You don't have to read fancy French philosophers like Jacques Derrida or the philosophical school called post-structuralism to know that.

Largely, we don't trust words because people are always trying to sell us something with their words. A credit card advertisement recently promised me, "Get the most of what you love." The most? Wow!

Then there was the foil wrapper on a piece of almond-filled dark chocolate which instructed me, "Keep believing in yourself and your special dreams." Yes, I will resolve to keep believing. Thank you, almond-filled dark chocolate. I was beginning to lose hope.

And then, shortly after I purchased a pair of brown leather clogs, I discovered the words on the soles, "Think fast, live slow." Hmmm, maybe I should slow down in life, but also think faster. That's life-changing.

So the soles of my brown clogs are preaching. A chocolate wrapper is trying to shape my worldview. And a credit card advertisement heralds the eschatological promise of providing most of what I love.

How does such language affect me? It makes me cynical about words, much less wise words and prophetic words. And I know I'm not alone. We live surrounded by so many money-mad marketers, salesman preachers, and humpty-dumpty heroes, that we're all a bit weary of words.

A Theology of Buzz

Still, words matter—and God's Word is what grows God's church. In the introduction, I described how, like an echo chamber, the Word reverberates through the life of the church, giving life to all its parts. Here's another analogy that helps me visualize the power of God's Word: God's Word gives life to a church like electricity gives power to a city.

Picture it. Electricity leaves the power plant and buzzes through power lines. Then it makes its way into street lights, grocery store freezers, office computers, and rows and rows of neighborhood homes. Lamps glow and refrigerators hum. In the same way, I'm contending that God's Word buzzes and hums through people and the local church, giving light to their eyes and hope to their hearts.

The problem is, we all know that words are unreliable and misleading. So how can it be that words give life? Words emblazoned on stone by God on Mt. Sinai are one thing, but how should we regard the evangelist on the airplane or the preacher in the pulpit?

We need to stop for a moment and consider the "little" vibrating thing itself—the Word. We need a theology of the buzz, because what I'm contending in this book is a faith proposition. Trusting God's Word to build our churches is an act of faith. Faith in God. Faith in His Word. And such faith is not natural, even for the Christian. It's supernatural. God must give it.

The "old man" in each of us—to use Paul's language—continually tempts us to value or build our churches on other things, things we can see and measure. We want to rely on marketing research, personal charisma, good music, or other natural devices. Now, I'm not saying that "natural" devices are bad, per se. But if we're relying upon them, there's no difference between us and the world. God means to challenge us right here. "Is not my word like fire," he would say to us, "and like a hammer that breaks the rock in pieces" (Jer. 23:29).

In this chapter, then, I'm going to make five statements that will be foundational for everything else in this book. If the reader wants to consider the following ideas more deeply, he or she can turn to the recommended reading that concludes the chapter. My understanding of Scripture on these matters has been instructed by these authors, especially Horton, Packer, and Ward. Furthermore, Scripture uses the phrase "Word of God" in a number of ways, but I will be using the phrase "God's Word" as synonymous with the Bible throughout the following discussion. When I use the phrase "God's words" I'm referring to His words more broadly.

Five Reliable Statements:
1. God's Word Is an Extension of God

The first thing to realize is that *God's Word is an extension of God Himself.* To hear His words that comprise the whole Bible is to hear Him. To obey His words is to obey Him. To ignore His words is to ignore Him. God "invests" Himself in His words, as Timothy Ward puts it. That is, God so identifies Himself with His words that our response to His words is our response to Him.

After King David slept with Bathsheba and killed her husband, God said to David, "You despised the word of the Lord," and in the next breath, "You have despised me" (2 Sam. 12:9–10; see also 1 Sam. 15:19, 23 in which Samuel rebuked King Saul).

Jesus, speaking to His disciples, identifies His words with Himself in the same way: "If anyone loves me, he will keep my word" (John 14:23a).

You can measure a person's opinion of God by his or her opinion of God's Word. That's why a person who loves God loves His Word, and the person who hates God rejects what God has spoken. God's Word is an extension of Himself— His identity, purposes, affections, and power.

Notice how the psalmist speaks of God's voice interchangeably with God Himself: "The voice of the Lord breaks the cedars; the Lord breaks the cedars of Lebanon. . . . The voice of the Lord shakes the wilderness; the Lord shakes the wilderness of Kadesh" (Psalm 29:5, 8). For God's voice to break or shake something is for God to break or shake something. The equation is simple.

Maybe too simple? Am I not just stating the obvious? After all, this is how we treat the words of the people we encounter every day. When I arrive home late at night from an elders' meeting after my wife has gone to bed, I know that the note of encouragement which she leaves taped to the bathroom mirror is an extension of her. And it warms my heart. It's not the paper or the ink lines that warm my heart, or even the conglomeration of letters d-e-a-r and l-o-v-e. It's the fact that my wife's affections—indeed, her soul's very bearing—become present through her use of words like "dear" and "love."

So, too, with the army captain's commands, the child's words of disgust at the dinner table, or the friend who tells us the time. In each case, the person is using the words to *do* something, and the action of speaking expresses some conviction, desire, or goal. It's an expression of his or her person.

Likewise, it may seem obvious that God's Word is an extension of Himself, but it's worth observing for at least three reasons. First, there has been a Satanic impulse inside each of us to separate God from His Word ever since the serpent said to Adam and Eve, "Did God actually say . . . ?" (Gen. 3:1). It's part of our fallen nature to say we love *Him* and yet give no heed to *His words* (cf. John 14:15; 1 John 5:3–4). We claim to love God, but how much time in the week do we spend reading the Bible? And do we prefer the preacher's exegesis or his personal stories?

Second, a host of twentieth-century theologies, like the serpent in Genesis 3, tried to separate God's Word from the

Bible. Some said the Bible merely "gives witness" to God's words. Some pitted Jesus against the Bible, saying that Jesus alone is the Word. Some leveled charges of "bibliolatry"—worshiping the Bible—against anyone who makes a big deal of the Bible. My goal here is not to argue substantively against such proposals, since I mean to be writing for people who believe the Bible is God's Word (see Ward or Horton's books at the end of the chapter for such a defense). However, I can assure you my wife would not be pleased if she e-mailed me at work and asked me to pick up five items at the store, but I picked up only three and explained, "I assumed your e-mail was merely 'giving witness' to your words, and that I was free to pick and choose from the list." As for the occasional charge of "bibliolatry," I am honestly not sure if a response is merited. People worshiping their Bibles—really? Has anyone seen people doing this?

God dwells with His people through His Word.

Third, there's a mystical impulse among many evangelicals that wants to close its eyes and simply experience God's presence and love. But imagine sitting next to a friend on a couch and saying, "Don't talk to me. I just want to feel your presence."

In Scripture, God communes with His people by communicating with them. Even God's Old Testament temple, the place where God is said to *dwell*, was distinguished from other ancient Near Eastern cultic temples because its most sacred spot contained not magical incantations for manipulating the gods into sending a good harvest or fertile wombs, but God's ten commandments, literally, His ten "words." God dwells with His people through His Word.

To read the Bible is not merely an exercise in intellectual

comprehension; it's an opportunity to stand before the throne of the King of the universe. It's an opportunity to encounter Him. God communes through communication.

Do you want to measure your regard for God? Then consider your regard for the Bible. It's Him addressing you and all the members of your church. It's Him drawing near with love and warning. Are you listening? Our attitude should be like Jeremiah's, who considered the false prophets of his day and trembled: "My heart is broken within me; all my bones shake; I am like a drunken man, like a man overcome by wine, because of the Lord and because of his holy words" (Jer. 23:9).

Five Reliable Statements:
2. God Acts through His Word

Evangelicals typically place their theological discussion of God's Word under the heading of "revelation." The Bible reveals God and His purposes to us, we say. It imparts information. And so we discuss the attributes of Scripture accordingly. We describe the Bible as inspired, authoritative, sufficient, inerrant, and clear. That is, the information it imparts is inspired, authoritative, and so forth. Such emphases make sense in light of the Enlightenment and post-Enlightenment's attack on Scripture's authority. God's people have responded to these challenges by rightly reinforcing their arguments for the propositional nature of Scripture.

I wholeheartedly affirm all of this. But now let's add another element, which the authors mentioned above have done so well. God not only reveals information through His Word, *God acts through His Word.* That's our second foundational statement. God acts when He speaks. He acts in three ways: He creates, He sustains, and He both establishes and breaks relationships.

God Creates with His Words

You and I create with hands, shovels, and bulldozers. But not God. God is Spirit, and He creates by speaking. He says, "Be," and it is. So the psalmist looks back on Genesis 1 and exclaims, "By the word of the Lord the heavens were made, and by the breath of his mouth all their host" (Ps. 33:6). The author of Hebrews agrees: "We understand that the universe was created by the word of God, so that what is seen was not made out of things that are visible" (Heb. 11:3). Invisible words create visible matter.

God Sustains the Universe with His Words

Scientists tell us that atoms and quarks, planets and suns, are held together by the mechanical laws of gravitation, electromagnetism, and strong and weak interaction. But think: Such laws are themselves the gusts of God's breath. They are words rolling off God's tongue second by second. As the author of Hebrews puts it, Jesus "upholds the universe by the word of his power" (Heb. 1:3)—by His buzzing and electric words. It's worth meditating for a moment on what actually happened when Jesus said to the wind and the waves, "Peace! Be still!" (Mark 4:39). Particles of nitrogen, oxygen, and hydrogen *listened*. Electrons and protons *obeyed*. Can you explain that?

God Establishes and Breaks Relationships through His Word

God made a verbal covenant with Abraham, and another one with Abraham's descendants, the Israelites. When they failed to keep that covenant, God exiled them. At every step, God's relationship with the people of Israel was established and broken by God's words.

Now, it's one thing to make this point in reference to the old covenant and the people of Israel. But the point becomes even more striking with the advent of the new covenant and the church. We're no longer talking about words written on tablets of stone, but, somehow, words written on human hearts. We're talking about the soul's very posture—its hopes and affections. It appears that, just as God created the universe with words, so He re-creates fallen hearts with words. He makes us "new creations." He "gives life to the dead and calls into existence the things that do not exist" (Rom. 4:17). The apostles speak in unison here:

- Peter reminds his Christian readers that they had been "born again . . . through the living and enduring word of God" (1 Peter 1:23).
- James says similarly that by God's "own will he brought us forth by the word of truth"; therefore, James exhorts his readers to "receive with meekness the implanted word, which is able to save your souls" (James 1:18, 21).
- John speaks of the Word that "abides in you" (1 John 2:14), and the truth that sets us free (John 8:32).
- Paul makes the parallel between God's work in creation and new creation explicit: "For God, who said, 'Let light shine out of darkness,' has shone in our hearts to give the light of the knowledge of the glory of God in the face of Jesus Christ" (2 Cor. 4:6). Elsewhere, he teaches "faith comes from hearing" (Rom. 10:17).

Of course, the apostles learned these promises from Jesus Himself, who said, "The words that I have spoken to you are spirit and life" (John 6:63b).

God's Word causes the new birth. It abides. It gives the knowledge of the glory of God in Christ. And God's Word can do all of this because it's "living and active" (Heb. 4:12). It buzzes and hums into the heart and turns on the light. Click! You can now see. You can now love God. Before, you couldn't.

Five Reliable Statements:
3. God Acts through His Word by His Spirit

But is this really the case? Again and again, God speaks to the Israelites, and they still disobey. Again and again, preachers preach the Bible while people yawn, fall asleep, or forget. Where are all those clicking lightbulbs and new-creation hearts?

This brings us to a third foundational sentence: *God acts through His Word by His Spirit.*

God's words have power because they move by God's Spirit and do exactly what the Spirit wishes. So Jesus told Nicodemus, "The wind blows where it wishes, and you hear its sound, but you do not know where it comes from or where it goes. So it is with everyone who is born of the Spirit" (John 3:8). Sometimes the Spirit uses God's words to harden a heart (Isa. 6:9–10; Matt. 13:14–15; Acts 28:26–27). Sometimes He uses them to soften one (Matt. 13:16; Acts 28:28; Rom. 15:18–21). But God's words always act according to the Spirit's will. He blows where He wishes.

The electrical operations of God's Word are not magical. They are spiritual. God's Spirit works together with God's Word. Here's Jesus putting it all together: "It is the Spirit who gives life; the flesh is no help at all. The words that I have spoken to you are spirit and life" (John 6:63). The Spirit's work is not contrasted with the work of Jesus' words in this passage; it's contrasted with the flesh's work—the kind of work accomplished by strength, beauty, or intelligence (see 2 Cor. 10:3). Jesus' words and the Spirit work together to give us spirit and life.

Perhaps the most vivid illustration of this in the Bible occurs in Ezekiel 36 and 37. In chapter 36, we encounter God's astounding new covenant promises:

And I will give you a new heart, and a new spirit I will put within you. And I will remove the heart of stone from your flesh and give you a heart of flesh. And I will put my Spirit within you, and cause you to walk in my statutes and be careful to obey my rules. (Ezek. 36:26–27)

God promises to give His people a new heart and a new spirit. He will do this by putting His Spirit within us.

How then will God do this? Ezekiel 37 contains the answer. The chapter begins with God giving the prophet a vision of standing in a valley of dry bones:

How does life come to those who are spiritually dead?

The hand of the Lord was upon me, and he brought me out in the Spirit of the Lord and set me down in the middle of the valley; it was full of bones. And he led me around among them, and behold, there were very many on the surface of the valley, and behold, they were very dry. (vv. 1–2)

The stage is set. Then comes the challenge: "And he said to me, 'Son of man, can these bones live?' And I answered, 'O Lord God, you know.'"

That, of course, is the question that should drive every Christian and every church leader—how does life come to those who are spiritually dead? God gives the first half of the answer by telling Ezekiel to preach:

Then he said to me, "Prophesy over these bones, and say to them, O dry bones, hear the word of the Lord. Thus says the Lord God to these bones: Behold, I will cause breath to enter you, and you shall live. And I will lay sinews upon you, and will cause flesh to come upon you, and cover you with skin, and put breath in you, and you shall live, and you shall know that I am the Lord."

So I prophesied as I was commanded. And as I prophesied, there was a sound, and behold, a rattling, and the bones came together, bone to its bone. And I looked, and behold, there were sinews on them, and flesh had come upon them, and skin had covered them. (vv. 4–8)

Ezekiel preached words, and life began to form. Bodies took shape. But more was needed. Words weren't enough. The next sentence reads, "But there was no breath in them." Keep in mind that the Hebrew word for both "breath" and "wind" is the same word for "spirit." The author seems interested in the double meaning as the story continues:

Then he said to me, "Prophesy to the breath [spirit]; prophesy, son of man, and say to the breath, Thus says the Lord God: Come from the four winds [spirits], O breath [spirit], and breathe on these slain, that they may live." So I prophesied as he commanded me, and the breath [spirit] came into them, and they lived and stood on their feet, an exceedingly great army. (vv. 9–10)

The passage is drenched with the word for "spirit," and the meaning can hardly be missed. God's Spirit joins God's preached word—a word preached through a man—to give spiritual life where there is spiritual death. This very interpretation is offered moments later, as the new covenant promise of chapter 36 is recalled:

> *Therefore prophesy, and say to them, Thus says the Lord*
> *God: Behold, I will open your graves and raise you from*
> *your graves, O my people. . . .And I will put my Spirit*
> *within you, and you shall live, and I will place you in your*
> *own land. Then you shall know that I am the Lord.*
> (vv. 12–14)

The power of God's Word is a faith proposition. It takes faith to believe that invisible words and the invisible Spirit could give life to a valley of dry bones. By comparison, it takes absolutely no faith to believe in the power of beauty, intelligence, strength, style, or humor. These qualities are attractive, and we can literally watch them draw a crowd. We can watch them build a "church."

The apostle Paul knew better. He knew that spiritual life is created through God's words and Spirit working together. He knew that the Thessalonian church was loved by God "because our gospel came to you not only in word, but also in power and in the Holy Spirit and with full conviction" (1 Thess. 1:5; see also 1 Cor. 2:4; Gal. 3:2–3). How did he know this? He had witnessed the change in their lives. Amid temptation, they were obedient. Amid persecution, they had joy. "You became imitators of us and of the Lord, for you received the word in much affliction, with the joy of the Holy Spirit, so that you became an example to all the believers in Macedonia and in Achaia" (1 Thess. 1:6–7). It's not surprising then that Paul would refer to the Word of God as the "sword of the Spirit" (Eph. 6:17).

There is no greater power a church has at its disposal than preaching the Father's Word of the Son working through the

Spirit. God's Word always accomplishes what God means it to accomplish, which brings us to a fourth statement.

Five Reliable Statements:
4. God's Word and Spirit
Act Together *Efficaciously*

God's Word and Spirit work together efficaciously. Combined, the Word and Spirit make a difference. This point has been implicit so far, but it's worth making explicit.

Our words are unstable, unreliable, and untrustworthy. Even when they are true, people will ignore or misunderstand us. They're just not effective. They don't get the job done. So we say things like "Money talks" or "Actions speak louder than words" or, as Theodore Roosevelt put it, "Speak softly and carry a big stick; you will go far."

God's Word doesn't fail. It accomplishes. It succeeds. Every time.

But God's words are different. They are *efficacious*. That is, they have their intended effect. Christians, as a matter of faith, must remember this. Listen to the prophet Isaiah, and pay attention especially to his verbal phrases:

For as the rain and the snow come down *from heaven and do not return there but water the earth,* making *it bring forth and sprout,* giving *seed to the sower and bread to the eater, so shall my word* be *that goes out from my mouth; it* shall not return *to me empty, but it* shall accomplish *that which I purpose, and* shall succeed *in the thing for which I sent it.* (Isa. 55:10–11, emphasis added; see also Ezek. 12:25)

Rainwater comes, makes, and gives. Droplets of water filter into the dirt, germinate seeds, and yield green shoots of life. Such is God's Word. It doesn't fail. It accomplishes. It succeeds. Every time. Maybe it hardens and maybe it softens, as we said earlier. But it accomplishes its will every time.

As Michael Horton has put it, God's Word does not merely impart information; it creates life. It's not only descriptive; it's effective. It produces worship, obedience, communion, and disciples.

When God speaks, some kind of change happens—always.

Five Reliable Statements:
5. God Speaks through
Human Preachers and Human Words

Finally, we come to a fifth statement, which may be the strangest and most surprising of all: *God speaks through human preachers and human words.*

It is one thing to look back at Genesis 1, read about God commanding light to appear, nod our heads, and affirm that God's words are powerful. It feels like another thing to say that what the preacher does on Sunday morning bears the same kind of power.

It's true that it would be downright silly to confuse our words with God's primordial words at creation, and just plain heretical to confuse our words with the words of inspired Scripture (see 2 Tim. 3:16; 2 Peter 1:19–21). Those all-important qualifications made, the Scriptures say again and again that God will speak with new-creation power as we faithfully expound the message of Scripture.

The Words of Jesus

Here are just a few examples from the New Testament, beginning with the words of Jesus.

When sending seventy-two disciples out to preach, Jesus tells them, "The one who *hears you hears me*, and the one who *rejects you rejects me*, and the one who rejects me rejects him who sent me" (Luke 10:16, all italics added).

After praying for His disciples, Jesus prays for future disciples: "I do not ask for these only, but also for those who will believe in me *through their word*" (John 17:20, italics added).

The Words of Paul, Peter, and John

Writing to the Thessalonians, Paul remarkably equates the words he preached with God's words: "And we also thank God constantly for this, that when you received the word of God, which you heard from us, you accepted it not as the word of men but as what it really is, the word of God, which is at work in you believers" (1 Thess. 2:13; also Gal. 1:11). Paul knew that God efficaciously works through preaching: "It pleased God through the folly of what we preach to save those who believe" (1 Cor. 1:21).

Peter also equates God's eternal, unchanging word with human preaching: "You have been born again, not of perishable seed but of imperishable, through the living and abiding word of God. . . .And this word is the good news that was preached to you" (1 Peter 1:23, 25). He is even more explicit later in the letter: "If anyone speaks, he should do it as one speaking the very words of God" (1 Peter 4:11 NIV).

John makes a similar equation: "Whoever knows God listens to us; whoever is not from God does not listen to us" (1 John 4:6).

God speaks through human preachers and human words. It's hard to believe, but that's why we must ask for faith:

• faith that encountering the Bible is encountering God;

- faith that God acts efficaciously through His Word by His Spirit; and
- faith that God puts this power to work when Christians like you and me speak.

Power for the Universe—and the Church

God's Word, working through God's Spirit, is the most powerful force in the universe and in the church. Father, Son, and Spirit wonderfully conspire to pour forth their power through speech, to accomplish their single will through words.

That's the theological foundation for the rest of this book. Our goal now is to trace the Word and Spirit's power from one area of the church's life to another, almost like we were following the flow of electricity through power lines from one building to the next.

The best place to begin, I believe, is with the heart of the individual person. What happens when the evangelist's invitation zaps the human heart? What do the electric reverberations of God's Word and Spirit look like in action? Furthermore, how should we view the apparent effectiveness that other things can have in persuading people, like good deeds or music or the style of a building's décor? These are the questions to which we now turn.

Recommended Reading

Adam, Peter. *Hearing God's Word: Exploring Biblical Spirituality.* ed. D. A. Carson. Downers Grove, Ill.: InterVarsity, 2004.

Horton, Michael S. *People and Place: A Covenant Ecclesiology.* Louisville, Ky.: Westminster John Knox, 2008. Chapters 2 and 3.

Packer J. I. *Knowing God.* London, England: Hodder and Stoughton, 1993. First published in 1973, chapter 6.

Thompson, Mark D. *A Clear and Present Word: The Clarity of Scripture.* ed. D. A. Carson. Downers Grove, Ill.: InterVarsity, 2006.

Ward, Timothy. *Words of Life: Scripture as the Living and Active Word of God.* Nottingham, England: InterVarsity, 2009.

3 } the word frees

It's hard to maintain faith in the power of God's Word.

How many times have I explained the good news of Jesus Christ to friends and strangers and then watched them . . . do nothing.

How many times have I stepped into the pulpit, my heart blooming with joy over the biblical text, preached my guts out, and then received only well-mannered "thank yous" from courteous faces moving quickly toward the door.

How many times have I found my own heart deadened to Scripture.

Faith is difficult because the operations of God's Word are not visible to the eyes. So pastors spend week after week in their studies hunched over new and older books, and year after year in the pulpit filling their mouths with God's even older words. But then they look out and see the same old faces staring back at them. They wonder why nothing seems to change. Some walk back to their offices, glance out the window, and watch as cranes half a mile away build the 5,000-seat auditorium for the trendy new church with large video screens and boy bands. You can almost hear the sigh.

God's Word and Something More

I recently heard about the pastors of one church who have struggled to maintain such faith in God's Word. Historically, these leaders were known for their commitment to the primacy of expositional preaching. They would stand up to read and preach the Bible with reverence, and a hush would come over the congregation. Ears would perk up. Fidgeting would stop.

But then something changed. They became discouraged by the lack of growth, and so they began a second service geared to a younger generation. The pastors changed their clothes between services. Some said they changed their hair. More gel? More spike?

More significantly, the church "lost its hush" whenever God's Word was read. That's how one departing member put it. Another departing member, himself known for stylish attire, grieved that the leaders began to confuse tattoos with "authenticity." Both of these members, like many others, left to find a church where God's Word was central.

On the one hand, it's easy to be sympathetic with the pastors. The apostle Paul said he would "become all things to all people" (1 Cor. 9:22), which some not surprisingly interpret as a mandate to dress, speak, sing, and even design buildings according to the customs of the people. These pastors, no doubt, had observed a number of generational changes and lovingly wanted to reach both a younger and an older crowd. I have no problem with hair gel or trendy shirts, and I certainly have no problem with big churches. May God fill all our churches!

What concerns me about this kind of scenario, however, is a possible lack of faith. There is an underlying assumption that God's Word alone "didn't work." It wasn't sufficient and needed a little help. The girl can't get a date wearing that plain old dress, so buy her something pretty and add more makeup.

We need to be careful about interpreting Paul's words to make him sound like a modern-day niche marketer. I understand why magazine publishers, car companies, and clothing retailers adjust their marketing campaigns to suit the natural appetites of various kinds of groups. It works. It gains customers. But does God really need to attract sinners in the same way? Also, I understand why insecure teenagers might care about the brands of their shirts. They want to appear "with it." But God's men in the pulpit?

Paul commended being all things to all men, but his point was that we should be willing to sacrifice personal preferences rather than cause people to stumble in spiritual matters. That's not the same thing as trying to gain hearers with designer jeans.

Furthermore, notice what happens when we try to "reach out" using such devices: Christ's people divide generationally and culturally. Lowering the walls for one group will raise them for another.

Now, having begun somewhat critically, let me admit there is a real conversation to have about the relationship between God's Word and other things Christians use in ministry. Even if we grant that God's Word working through God's Spirit is uniquely powerful to create spiritual life, how do we relate Word ministry and various forms of deed ministry, like hospitality or caring for the poor? How important is the style of music in a church, or a preacher's style of clothes? What about a preacher's charisma or sense of humor? How important is the church building?

Before we can answer these questions, we need to look at what happens when the electric current of God's Word and Spirit enters the ears and makes its way through the individual person. Once we see what the Word and Spirit alone can do to give life and freedom to the individual, we will be in a better position to understand what role is played by music or good deeds or even spiky hair. Those are the two goals of this chapter: Consider what the Word does when encountering the human heart, and then compare this with other aspects of ministry.

Brian's Risky Trips

Before he joined my church, Brian surrendered almost a decade of his life to drug addiction. He has a number of stories from those days, but one memory in particular struck me as he shared his testimony. He recalled routine two a.m. trips with friends to a rough area of Baltimore to buy drugs—sometimes cocaine, sometimes heroin, sometimes marijuana. The trips were risky. He had seen a number of friends beat up or arrested. So while his friends drove, he would sit quietly in the back seat, praying under his breath that God would protect him. Brian's parents had taught him the gospel, and he had made a profession of faith himself. But now he was sunk into full-time addiction.

He said of the drug runs, "I was petrified. But it was never enough for me to tell them to pull over and get out of the car. I couldn't break the addiction." So he would pray, "God I know this is wrong, but let me get out of the city tonight without getting beat up, without getting robbed, or worse."

The picture of Brian praying on the way to get drugs struck me for two reasons. First, I could identify with it. I'm a sinner.

I've never been addicted to drugs, but I've been addicted to other sins, like pride or vanity. I know what it is to choose something even while I know it's harming me. Second, it's a perfect picture of the enslavement of sin. A temptation looms before you, and you know better than to say yes, but you grab it anyway. You can't help it. The promise of pleasure persuades you that any trouble will be worth it.

The Enslaved Heart

Sin is indeed an enslaver. It binds the heart to wanting the wrong things. It convinces the heart that God's truth is a lie, and that sin offers greater pleasure than God.

The frightening thing is, we're all born slaves to sin. As Jesus put it, "I tell you the truth, everyone who sins is a slave to sin" (John 8:34 NIV). From birth, that's all of us!

This metaphor of slavery is worth meditating on. Picture yourself as a slave. It would mean you are owned by someone else, and you would have to do that owner's bidding. You would not be free to do as you please. To really get the picture, you could imagine a chain around your neck and the owner holding the other end of the chain. He could pull you wherever he wanted to go, and you could not do otherwise. You would have no real choice, because your will would be coerced. You would be stuck.

Sin doesn't place its chain around your neck, but around your heart— its desires.

Now here's something astonishing. According to the Bible, sin doesn't place its chain around your neck but around your heart—its affections, desires, and beliefs. And it's not someone else holding the chain. It's you! It's your own sinful nature. Apart from Christ, your sinful nature owns you, requiring your will to move whichever way it pleases. You want what your sinful nature *wants*. Every time. All the time. Your heart is not free to do otherwise. It's stuck.

Our problem isn't located at the level of our will, as if to say the root problem is that we keep *choosing* wrong things. Our problem is located in our nature, which is corrupt and sinful. So just as an apple tree bears apples according to its nature, and a lion chooses to eat meat according to its nature, so a sinner always chooses sin according to his or her nature.

What's a sinful nature? It's a nature that has deposed God as God. It's unable to acknowledge that God deserves His throne, because it's convinced it belongs in His chair. Now, the sinful nature might "believe in God" and decide to keep the old man around for useful employment, like getting one out of tight spots. The sinful nature might even attempt to obey God's law as a way of proving that one's as good as He is. The point is, the sinful nature is utterly unable to love God more than oneself, to desire God's glory, and to joyfully embrace His rule. You might as well ask an apple tree to bear oranges, or a lion to eat grass. Here's how Paul puts it: "For the mind that is set on the flesh is hostile to God, for it does not submit to God's law; indeed, it cannot" (Rom. 8:7). This means that even the "good" actions of the sinful nature are, therefore, corrupt; they're motivated by the love of self and not God (Isa. 64:6).

"The heart wants what it wants," said Woody Allen when asked why he had committed adultery. And the heart of our slavery is the fact that our fallen natures are enslaved to believing that we are God. And all our loves and all our actions follow accordingly.

What Cannot Free the Heart

This metaphor of slavery is worth meditating on, as I say, because churches need to know what they're up against. (It would be just as valuable to meditate on other biblical metaphors for describing our spiritual condition like "dead" or "blind" or "deaf." But we'll stick with the metaphor of slavery for now.) They are not up against the need to *change people's minds* about God, like a political campaign tries to change the public's mind about a candidate, or a marketing campaign tries to change people's minds about a product. If the challenge were that simple, it would make sense for churches to mimic the methods of political and marketing campaigns.

Can we attract people with the right style of clothes? Of course. Can we cause them to feel rapturous emotions with modulated music? Yes. Can we elicit gratitude through acts of mercy? Again, yes. Can we win their approval with humor, and their affections with kindness? Indeed. Can we even cause them to be moral with the right combination of legal incentives and disincentives? Sure. We change our minds about other people all the time: "I didn't like him at first, but now I do."

But when we're dealing with changing a sinful nature, we're dealing with something categorically different. To borrow from Jeremiah, we're asking the leopard to change its spots (Jer. 13:23). To borrow from Jesus, we're asking a bad tree to bear good fruit or the thorn bush to bear figs (Luke 6:43–44). What humans need is not a change of mind about God, but a change of nature. They need to be born again, given spiritual sight, set free. Music can't do that. Style can't do that. Law and good deeds cannot do that. We need something not with natural power but something with divine power. Paul writes, "For though we walk in the flesh, we are not waging war according to the flesh. For the weapons of our warfare are not of the flesh but have divine power to destroy strongholds" (2 Cor. 10:3–4).

What's strange is, you can "talk theology" with church leaders, and many will acknowledge everything I just said about our enslavement to sin and the depth of our problem as fallen sinners. But turn the conversation to local church practices, and that earlier conversation gets left behind. They begin to talk about reaching out with the right style of music, or dimming the lights to create the right worship effect. They readily adopt the devices of the marketing firm or the political campaign, even though such devices are utterly powerless to change the nature of the heart.

What Can Free the Heart?

What frees an enslaved heart? Only one thing: the truth of God's Word working with the Holy Spirit. As Jesus said, "You will know the truth, and the truth will set you free" (John 8:32). The truth comes, and the Spirit enlivens the heart toward that truth. He electrifies what's dead. He gives the heart "eyes" to see it (Eph. 1:18), as well as the ability to recognize its significance, to value it properly, and to love it. The person is now free, because his heart is now properly conformed to God's truth.

Picture the operations of God's truth or Word like DNA replacement therapy, as if your body had "bad DNA" that could somehow be replaced with "good DNA." Or think of reprogramming a corrupted computer. The old computer coding constantly crashes the computer; it needs to be reprogrammed. This is what God's truth does for a person's nature, heart, and will—it replaces the bad DNA or bad coding with good. The person is now free to operate as he or she was designed to operate. Love and good works begin to abound.

This confrontation between truth and untruth is where the decisive battle happens for heart change. Untruth can only be defeated and replaced through a confrontation with Truth. Here's how the story goes: It begins with a sham king sitting upon a sham throne, convinced that all glory and rule are his. That's all of us in our fallen nature. Then an ambassador for the real king enters the cardboard throne room and speaks a simple word: "The real king is coming. He's willing to forgive. Surrender."

This is the all-important moment. This is where the battle is won or lost. Truth is staring Untruth in the face, and everyone watching wants to know, Will the sham king listen or won't he? If the Spirit electrifies his ears, eyes, and heart so that he can hear, see, and love, then, yes, he will listen, repent, and believe. He'll climb out of his paper chair and bow with unfeigned love and worship (see Phil. 3:3). If the Spirit doesn't, then he won't. Period.

Suppose, however, the ambassador decides to soften the real king's words. He doesn't tell the sham king to surrender. He tells him instead that he can offer him "a great opportunity for an alliance" with the true king. Meanwhile, he plays a little mood music. He tells sweet stories. He does everything he can to flatter the imposter with affirmations of his humanity. Would the ambassador make any progress this way? Maybe. He might even get this pathetic and naked emperor to declare himself a friend of the real king. Of course, the whole affair would only reinforce the sham because there would be no real surrender. The ambassador will have succeeded only in creating a *nominal* Christian.

Only the power of God's Word and Spirit can give true freedom—the freedom of obedience, the freedom of righteousness, the freedom of joyful conformity to the character of God (see Romans 6–8). After all, only the Word and Spirit can replace one nature with another. They destroy the old and create the new. Their power is awesome. They pulverize the hard heart like a massive asteroid colliding with a planet. Paul could, therefore, say to a group of Christians, "But thanks be to God, that you who were once slaves of sin have become obedient from the heart to the standard of teaching to which you were committed" (Rom. 6:17; also 1 Peter 2:16).

Priority of Spirit-Filled Word Ministry

If the individual heart is freed and given life exclusively through the Word, then priority in the local church must go to Word ministry—sharing the Word, preaching the Word, singing the Word, reading the Word, and praying the Word. This is Paul's conclusion in 2 Corinthians after comparing the Spiritless old covenant with a Spirit-filled new covenant. Where the Spirit of Christ is present, Paul says, "there is freedom" (3:17). The Spirit transforms fallen sinners into the image of Christ as they behold Christ's face and become free (3:18).

But how do they see Christ's face? They see with their ears. Paul writes:

> *We have renounced disgraceful, underhanded ways. We refuse to practice cunning or to tamper with God's word,* but by the open statement of the truth *we would commend ourselves to everyone's conscience in the sight of God.* (4:2, emphasis added)

Christians and church leaders must set forth God's truth plainly. If people reject this truth, it's not because of inadequate market research. They reject it for other reasons:

And even if our gospel is veiled, it is veiled only to those who are perishing. In their case the god of this world has blinded the minds of the unbelievers, to keep them from seeing the light of the gospel of the glory of Christ, who is the image of God. For what we proclaim is not ourselves, but Jesus Christ as Lord, with ourselves as your servants for Jesus' sake. (4:3–5)

Paul knows that any rejection of his message is a spiritual matter. People reject Christ's lordship because they remain firmly ensconced on their paper thrones. Their hearts are darkened and blind to God's reality. The good news is, the Spirit comes and changes hearts through "open-statement-of-the-truth" ministry. He frees them by creating them anew.

Paul continues: "For God, who said, 'Let light shine out of darkness,' has shone in our hearts to give the light of the knowledge of the glory of God in the face of Jesus Christ" (4:6).

Let there be light! Bang! A whole new universe. A whole new creation. A whole new nature. *That's* the power needed to free sinners.

Strangely, church leaders get caught up in all kinds of power for building their churches: the power of ethnic and cultural affinity, the power of entertainment, the power of rhetoric and humor, the power of good organizational principles, and so much more. But does any power in the universe match God's power to breathe out worlds or dismiss death simply with words? "Let there be light!" and "Lazarus, come forth!"? No; there is nothing like it. Yet this same power is available to the preacher through God's Word. This is why people get converted when listening to anonymous radio broadcasts, or even listening to hypocritical preachers who preach "in pretence" (Phil. 1:18). Relying on anything else indicates a dramatic failure to recognize how radically new the new creation is.

What about Everything Else?

But surely we don't want to license hypocritical preaching. A preacher's life must play some role, right? What role?

This brings us to our second main topic for our chapter: How do we understand the relationship between the Word's unique power and the host of other factors that seem to play a role in a ministry's outward success? For instance, some preachers have greater natural gifts of charisma, humor, or eloquence than others. Even the Bible acknowledges this (see Acts 18:24; 2 Cor. 8:18). Why then does it seem that such preachers yield a greater harvest if indeed the Word works by supernatural power? Also, how should we regard the seeker-sensitive or contextualizing impulse to "meet people where they're at" with the right style of music, dress, or building décor? And how important are deed ministries like hospitality and caring for the poor relative to the Word ministries of preaching and evangelism?

Some church leaders criticize giving primacy to the role of preaching and evangelism, as I have done here. For instance, they might observe that God gave His Old Testament people prophets, priests, and kings, and Jesus came as all three. The prophetic work of preaching and evangelism is important, it's said, but we must not arbitrarily privilege it over the kingly work of administration and program-building, or the priestly work of relationship-building and care-giving.

Other leaders say that *deed ministry* is no less important than *Word ministry*. Both are needed like a bird needs two wings to fly.

I'm grateful for the renewed emphasis on good works and other elements. But we still need to respect the unique role of God's Word in creating new life and setting captives free. My worry is that the analogies of two wings or prophet/priest/king wrongly characterize the relationship between the Word and these other things by making these other things equally important. The analogies are compelling because they are simple and clear, but they don't match the biblical data. Let me explain why by offering two alternative analogies—the analogy of a platform and the analogy of evidence.

A Platform for the Word

Most of the things mentioned above provide an opportunity for the Word to do its work; that is, they build *a platform* on which the Word speaks. This platform always supports the Word ministry. For example:

- Church buildings, especially well-designed and administered ones, provide the opportunity for people to conveniently gather and hear God's Word preached and taught.
- Points of social, cultural, and ethnic connection provide the opportunity to reach more people with God's Word, because, generally speaking, more people will attend a meeting of any kind—including a church meeting—that feels socially, culturally, or ethnically familiar.
- A preacher's eloquence, humor, and charisma provide opportunities to proclaim the Word clearly. Frankly, good looks and fashion sense might do this as well. More people prefer to hear an attractive, charismatic speaker than a boring and plain one.
- Playing music in a culturally familiar style lowers social barriers and increases people's comfort levels, which in turn helps to make the notes and melodies a better platform for the words of Scripture.

- The ability to build strong relationships and develop community provides opportunities because people are generally more inclined to listen to those whom they know and trust.
- Financial resources provide opportunities to present God's Word. Money builds buildings, buys airplane tickets, and feeds the children of missionaries.
- Acts of kindness and goodness by God's people can make the message of the Scriptures attractive and even compelling.

Being human means facing the debris-filled whirlwinds of physical, cultural, emotional, relational, financial, and moral realities. Such realities can hinder Word ministry, or they can be employed to build a platform for it. This should be as obvious as saying a big building holds more people than does a small one. God can and does use natural means to spread His Word, including the means of marketing firms and political campaigns. All things being equal, we can say that the greater level of natural gifting or natural affinity, the greater opportunity there is to speak God's Word. For ministers and churches, then, Jesus' parable of the talents is relevant here: the servant with five talents *should* employ his five talents, the servant with two his two, and the servant with one his one (Matt. 25:14–30). We have a stewardship obligation to maximize our natural resources and gifts for supernatural ends.

Yet my sense is that this is where the conversation ends for many church leaders. Their rationale is, if something provides an opportunity, grab it! The problem is, Scripture and life often give us a number of factors to consider, and wisdom requires us to temper one set of considerations with others. Let me offer three further considerations.

Retain Prudence

First, to say that these things are "platforms" or "opportunity-providers" means that they fall into the realm of prudence. Not every opportunity to speak God's Word is a good opportunity. Some come with costs. Even matters commanded by Scripture, as with the command "Let us do good to everyone" (Gal. 6:10), are subject to principles of Christian liberty and circumstance (which is why Paul precedes this command with the words "as we have opportunity"). We should not assume that every opportunity, by definition, is good. Discretion must always be used. The Word alone gives spiritual life, which means it alone must play the lead role. Everything else, at most, plays supporting cast and is subject to other considerations. The problem with comparing ministry to *two equal wings* or *three equal offices* is that it tempts churches to build their ministries upon these other things, as if they could equally give life.

Unite around the Gospel

Second, the temptation to give a lead role to something besides the Word risks undermining the gospel. The church of Christ is to be united around the gospel words of Christ, not around ethnicity, socioeconomic class, age, style, or anything else. It's where there is neither Jew nor Greek, slave nor free, male nor female, because the gospel creates one new man among those who were formerly divided (Gal. 3:28; Eph. 2:19–20). Consider carefully, therefore, what it means when we deliberately attempt to unite people to our church, not around the gospel Word, but around some point of natural affinity. Whether we mean to or not, we're sending the message that (1) the gospel Word is not sufficient for creating unity among sinners; and that (2) other forms of natural unity are just as worthy as gospel unity.

Most church leaders, I assume, aren't thinking this way. They're thinking that they can draw outsiders through the door with something like style, intellectual sophistication, or a worship experience, but then they'll give them the Word. To my knowledge, nobody is actually saying "Let's save sinners and build a church with the style of our clothes."

They might be doing this unawares. But at best, they are sending mixed messages. Think about it: The Word that the church offers is not a magical word like "abracadabra"—just get them through the door, say the magic word, and "Poof!" they're saved. No, it's the Word of *justification* and *alien righteousness*. It's the promise that "you can gain the merit of Christ and the favor of God Himself not because of your dress, your intelligence, or your Sunday school attendance. Instead, through faith in Christ's redeeming sacrifice, you will be declared worthy."

What happens then when a local church tries to reach its community by saying, "We're smart and hip, too. So join us"? It subtly undermines the very message of the justification by faith and the free gift of righteousness because it invests value in hipness to unify people.

Like the laws of Sinai that divided Israel from the nations, so this world divides itself according to laws of fashion, the laws of funny, the laws of intellectual sophistication, and the laws of ethnic belonging. And people seek worth and favor by trying to live up to those laws: "I want to feel good about myself because of the way I dress, and I want to be around other people who dress well, because that will say good things about me." Call it "justification by style" or "justification by intellectual sophistication" or "justification by ethnicity." When you, therefore, say to the world, "Hey, don't count us among the uncool, but count us among the cool," you merely play into the hands of the world's systems of law, justification, and separation of the "righteous" and the "unrighteous." People *will* come to your church, but you'll have a church full of Pharisees—style Pharisees, ethnic Pharisees, music Pharisees, and more. Perhaps this is why you will not find a single verse in the Bible that commends drawing outsiders toward God's people through anything other than the gospel or a gospel-changed life. As the adage goes, what you win them with, you win them to.

To put it another way, trying to unite or attract people to my church through some point of natural affinity or gifting means I'm potentially relying on the power of people's idols to build my church.

Now, there's a word here for conservative traditionalists as well. Many traditional churches are not saying "We'll get them with style." But they do have expectations about style once you show up for the Sunday gathering. "Wear your Sunday best because God is *pleeeeased* when we dress up." No, He's not (Ps. 51:16–17; Joel 2:13). Saying so is anti-gospel.

The point, finally, is that neither style, nor intelligence, nor ethnicity, nor anything else in all creation can separate people from the love of God in Christ. Therefore, we should not let them separate people from the love of the church. Our message on these issues must be, "It doesn't matter. Do what you will, and be what you are."

What will I as a church leader wear? Hopefully, something that people won't pay any attention to at all—something that will neither attract nor distract.

> *Worship, very simply, is born of repentance.*

One last strategy that risks undermining the gospel is the strategy of appealing to non-Christians by drawing them into the *experience* of worship. The goal here is to let outsiders *feel* what worshiping

God is like. The problem, however, is that worship is not a feeling or an experience. You cannot create true worship in people's hearts by placing them in the right surroundings. You might as well take them to the temple, have them sacrifice a lamb, and see if that doesn't provoke contrition in their hearts. A good percentage of the Old Testament is devoted to demonstrating that placing people in the right environment—in the land, under a king, with the law in hand—does not produce worshipers.

Worship, very simply, is born of repentance. It's the result of a Word- and Spirit-induced change of nature. The unrepentant, by definition, neither worship nor experience worship. The irony of so many hip and progressive churches is that they are relying on an old covenant mentality.

Remain Humble and Rely on God

Third, God often uses the weak, the poor, and the unlikely to attract sinners to Himself. He does this to show that power belongs to Him. Points of natural affinity, natural giftedness, and natural resources do indeed provide a platform or opportunity to speak the gospel. But right in the face of these sociological realities, God has a consistent track record of using the weak and the unlikely to show that power ultimately belongs to Him. In Genesis, He chooses the second-born son, not the first. In Exodus, He chooses stammering Moses to lead His people. In Deuteronomy, He tells Israel that He chose them in spite of the fact that they were the fewest of people and not the greatest (Deut. 7:7). In Samuel, He chooses the seventh son of Jesse, David, because "the Lord sees not as man sees: man looks on the outward appearance, but the Lord looks on the heart" (1 Sam. 16:7).

While exalting those of humble circumstance, God also humbles the exalted: the builders of Babel, Pharaoh, Sennacherib, Nebuchadnezzar, and so on. And so it goes through the Bible. Jesus Himself "had no form or majesty . . . no beauty that we should desire him" (Isa. 53:2). And of course Paul tells the church in Corinth:

> *Not many of you were wise according to worldly standards, not many were powerful, not many were of noble birth. But God chose what is foolish in the world to shame the wise; God chose what is weak in the world to shame the strong; God chose what is low and despised in the world, even things that are not, to bring to nothing things that are, so that no human being might boast in the presence of God.* (1 Cor. 1:26–29)

There's no room here for social-status Phariseeism or any other form of pride. Church leaders today are quick to lean into their strengths for building churches. To some extent, this must be appropriate. But how many, with Paul, boast all the more gladly of their weaknesses, so that the power of Christ would rest upon them (2 Cor. 12:9)?

There's a difference between removing distractions . . . and creating attractions.

Again, points of natural affinity, giftedness, and resources provide opportunities for the Word to go forth, but we must be careful not to build our churches upon such things. Let me offer one practical principle: There's a difference between *removing distractions* (uncomfortable seats, hot rooms, strange music, cultural or spiritual offenses) so that the Word is free to do its work; and *creating attractions* (through clothes, musical style, drama, etc.). Removing distractions, which is what

Paul does, is prudent; creating attractions, generally, is not. In my opinion, that means

- *Clothing:* We should choose clothing that (1) does not draw attention to ourselves and (2) shows respect for others. We should not choose clothes in order to impress.
- *Humor:* A dash of humor in the pulpit can help to lower emotional defenses, as well as to express genuine God-imaging joy in some application of the Word. We should not use humor to attract, impress, or win hearers.
- *Music:* I believe music provides a God-given avenue for the mind and heart to respond to God's revelation—to confess, to grieve, to rejoice, and to revel in His attributes (see chapter 8 for further discussion). We should not use music to create the *sense* or *experience* of worshiping God among the unrepentant. They, by definition, cannot worship. Nor should we use music to gain "customers."
- *Intelligence/charisma/eloquence:* Such gifts are wonderfully employed to convey the glory and beauty of God in the gospel, and they should be stewarded accordingly. So expect charismatic preachers to have bigger churches. But such gifts should not be used to impress or manipulate. The difference between a right and wrong use of eloquence, for instance, shows up in a thousand small decisions about which words to use. It's the difference, perhaps, between clear, strong, compelling images and flowery, erudite grandiloquence.
- *Relationships/community/good works:* Relationships and good works should be used to give evidence of the power of the message (the topic I move to next). They must not be used to supplant the message.

In sum, we should use whatever gifts, resources, and natural affinities we have to proclaim His Word, but we should also do our best to make sure people join our local church because they love the gospel, not because we're the cool church or the intellectual church, the baby-boomer church or the church of a particular ethnicity. Earlier I said that the greater the natural gift or natural affinity, the greater opportunity there is to speak God's Word. That's true. But it's also true that the greater the natural gift or affinity, the greater the risk. There's a risk to the Christian who will be tempted to rely on these natural advantages, and there's a risk to the non-Christian who stands a higher chance of being deceived into thinking he's a Christian, to his eternal loss. Hence, the talented, well-resourced church may have to work harder than others at walking by faith and doing what they can to prevent false professions. The naturally charismatic speaker might learn to refrain from playing on people's emotions, and the naturally funny speaker might learn how to hold in a joke or two.

Sadly, I find it's the case that the most talented preachers and well-resourced churches are often the most careless about cultivating seedbeds of Christian nominalism, when it should be the opposite.

Evidence for the Power of the Word

In addition to providing a platform or opportunity for the Word to go forth, several elements can provide evidence of the power of the Word. They confirm or testify to its life-changing power. The attractive nature of good works and the compelling picture of a Christian community are two such elements and they are endorsed in God's Word.

God does mean for some things to be *attractive* to the world, namely, the holiness and self-sacrificial love of Christians in their lives together and apart. The New Testament is filled with such statements:

> *So that they may see your good works and give glory to your Father who is in heaven.* (Matt. 5:16)
>
> *By this all people will know that you are my disciples, if you have love for one another.* (John 13:35)
>
> *Slaves . . .are to be well-pleasing, not argumentative, not pilfering, but showing all good faith, so that in everything they may adorn the doctrine of God our Savior.* (Titus 2:9–10)
>
> *Keep your conduct among the Gentiles honorable, so that when they speak against you as evildoers, they may see your good deeds and glorify God on the day of visitation.* (1 Peter 2:12)
>
> *Wives, be subject to your own husbands, so that even if some do not obey the word, they may be won without a word by the conduct of their wives—when they see your respectful and pure conduct.* (1 Peter 3:1–2)

I like the phrase Paul uses in Titus 2: Our good deeds and righteousness should *adorn* our doctrine. Maybe the girl does need to be dressed up after all; but we need to dress her only with righteousness and love, not designer jeans.

Does this mean that we should say that good works—like faithful marriages, honesty at work, caring for the poor, pursuing justice, submitting to non-Christian husbands—are *necessary* for conversion and church growth? Does it mean that the bird won't fly without the two wings of Word ministry and deed ministry?

It depends on what you mean by "necessary." Are good works necessary for the Word and Spirit to give new life? Certainly not! The previous chapter and the first half of this chapter should have dispensed with that idea. People get saved listening to hypocritical preachers and anonymous radio preachers. You can proclaim the gospel without deeds, but you cannot proclaim the gospel without words.

But aren't good deeds necessary for preserving the public reputation of the church and its Lord? For demonstrating that He means what He says? For demonstrating that we have integrity? Generally speaking, yes! Listen to how one biblical minister advises another: "Show yourself in all respects to be a model of good works, and in your teaching show integrity, dignity, and sound speech that cannot be condemned, so that an opponent may be put to shame, having nothing evil to say about us" (Titus 2:7–8).

The gospel Word creates gospel life in an individual and in a church. When that individual and church then turn to minister to others, their word and life should be *integrated*—have *integrity*. In one sense, there are not two things (two wings) but one thing with two distinct parts—a faithful witness in word and deed. Also—and this is very important—the two distinct parts are doing distinct things, unlike two wings. The Word is doing things that the deed cannot do: It's pointing to an invisible God who has sent His Son to die on the cross; it's calling all to repentance; it's freeing the enslaved; and it's giving life to the dead. The deed is then doing something the Word cannot do: It's demonstrating or picturing the effects of this gospel Word. It's testifying to its life-changing power. The Word is the main character; the deed is the supporting character.

To summarize: Are deeds "necessary" for raising the dead and freeing the enslaved? From the standpoint of the Spirit's work, no. From the standpoint of Christianity's public credibility, generally yes. The Spirit's work *will* produce evidence in our deeds. And every good deed becomes one more witness who testifies on behalf of the gospel's truth and power.

There's one related point to make here on matters of style. Whereas I don't believe we should *build* churches on styles of music or dress, I do believe that churches can do well to adjust their styles of music and dress for the sake of *loving* their members. For instance, I've heard White church leaders encourage other White church leaders to employ musical styles that would be more familiar to African Americans in order to build a multi-ethnic church. Multi-ethnic churches are wonderful, no doubt, but you never hear the apostles saying that unity between different ethnicities will come through musical style. True unity is only found through preaching the gospel (Gal. 3:26-29)! So *build* on the gospel only. On the other hand, I would, in some circumstances, advise largely White churches to *love* their Black members by seeking to diversify their worship style, as a deed-driven expression of faith and love. The gospel alone creates unity. Start there. Then, watch how the gospel creates a love which should in turn prompt us to sacrifice our own cultural preferences.

From One Slave to Another

The Word frees the heart, and it does so in the most remarkable way. Sarah, a member of my church who recently returned from two years in a largely Muslim Middle Eastern nation, knows this. She was there to evangelize, but it's hard to imagine someone with more social forces stacked against her. As a female, she didn't have the respect of most Muslim men. As a single female living away from her family, many Muslims suspected her of being immoral. Being an American exacerbated that suspicion. And as an American of Filipino descent, she was regarded as an indentured servant, since many Filipinos in that nation are.

Sarah's gospel work, in other words, had to occur through these many layers of discrimination. In one letter, she described being "mistaken for a house servant or prostitute everywhere I go."

Midway through her time overseas, Sarah sent the following e-mail to me and the other elders of our church. (I've removed the place names.) Sarah writes,

"I was so bad," Ida cried as she lay in her hospital bed. On the night before her hip replacement surgery, Ida shared her life story with much sorrow, as I watched the Lord break her heart of stone before my eyes. She comes from a long history of struggles: adultery, drug addiction, alcoholism, prostitution, abortion. She moved to [country name] in hopes of escaping her problems in the Philippines to work as a house maid, yet she only found herself trapped by wicked employers who physically and sexually abused her then later imprisoned her. Though Ida is still married with three children in the Philippines, she married a local man in this country to have a roof above her head and a little food on her plate. Ida is his first wife, as he is many years younger than her. However, he is now looking for a local woman to marry as his second wife to fulfill his family duties. Ida disapproves of this idea, yet her husband has already threatened to kill her if she would dare leave (and shame) him. It's true, her life is a mess.

Yet it utterly astounds me that no matter the situation, no matter how big, complicated, and twisted Ida's problems are, no matter how ugly her life had become, the lovingkindness, compassion, mercy, patience, and beauty of our Lord Jesus ever ABOUNDS! Indeed His light shines in the darkness, and the darkness cannot overcome it, amen and amen! No one is ever too far from the reach of our God—not us, not Ida! Ida shared the guilt she has been carrying for years, and she knew she needed to be forgiven but didn't know how God could ever forgive someone like her. What a sweet privilege it was and still is to proclaim the excellencies of Christ, to speak of His love, grace, and sufficiency of His sacrifice at the cross. What a sweet gift it is to tell her of the God who gives new, abundant, everlasting life, who died and rose again to pay our debts and bring us to God. What a joy it is to tell her about a different Way of life, that is the Way of Jesus. That it is not an easy Way, it may even make life more difficult for her as opposition will come, but His Way is exceedingly worth it all, no matter what. As we talked, read from the Word, and prayed together, it became clear to me that the Holy Spirit had taken hold of this broken woman, and He was not going to let her go.

Ida and I have been meeting at her home, as she is still recovering from the surgery. It excites me to watch the Lord work in her heart and mind, as He gives her a deeper hunger and thirst for Him. She loves listening to the audio Tagalog Bible and reading the Arabic-English Bible I gave her. She continues to ask many questions about how living the Way of Christ applies to her specific life situations. She excitedly told me how she was recently sitting on her bed with the Bible in her hand. She prayed to God, "Please give me food for my soul today." She just so "happened" to open her Bible to James 1:21–25 that spoke loud volumes to her about sin patterns that needed to be broken in her life. Praise God for His living and active Word that Ida would be a woman who lives by the very Word of God. Ask that God would grant me wisdom in knowing the state of her soul and encouraging her to get grounded in His Word, finding a church family, and living in obedience to our Master.

Ida is one of many thousands of Filipinas in [city name] who suffer through similar circumstances. Please intercede on their behalf, that they would know God is near the oppressed and brokenhearted and leave vengeance for the Lord to repay . . .

Thank you once again for allowing me to serve Him in this country. It is a privilege to watch the Lord captivate the hearts and minds of people in this city. Please keep praying for His mercy, as I am hopeful there is a harvest yet to come. . . .

> I love you all dearly!
> For His name's sake,
> Sarah

Did the Lord use their shared Filipino background to establish a connection? And their shared experience of being women? Presumably, yes. God does use natural means, and we should take advantage of them as occasion permits.

At the same time, Sarah understands something that many church leaders do not: The battle is far more intense than anything a little contextualizing can address. She understands that things like hair gel and designer jeans cannot convert the heart of a poverty-stricken, substance-addicted foreign woman enslaved in a wrongful second marriage. She understands that style and youth appeal do not cause a battered and hard-hearted woman to expose herself to further possible persecution for the sake of Jesus' name.

Instead, Sarah rejoices that a translated Bible does all that!

She can't keep from singing because she, a slave of Christ, can stammer out gospel words in her broken Filipino. Then Jesus will use those words to radically free the heart of a different kind of slave. "For the weapons of our warfare are not of the flesh but have divine power to destroy strongholds" (2 Cor. 10:4).

And Brian, the former drug addict—how's he doing? Amazing! He leads our church's involvement in a nearby homeless shelter, getting our members to do everything from serving meals to leading chapel services. The man knows the gospel, loves the gospel, submits to the gospel, and so adorns it continually. Praise God, he's free!

Recommended Reading

Dever, Mark. *Nine Marks of a Healthy Church*. Wheaton, Ill.: Crossway, 2004.

Guinness, Os. *Dining with the Devil*. Grand Rapids: Baker, 1993.

Wells, David. *Courage to Be Protestant*. Grand Rapids: Eerdmans, 2008.

White, Thomas and John M. Yeats. *Franchising McChurch: Feeding Our Obsession with Easy Christianity*. Colorado Springs: David C. Cook, 2009.

4} the word gathers

It's Sunday morning, and you're walking into a church for the very first time.

You step into some type of foyer and someone briefly greets you. Maybe it's his job. Maybe he's just nice. Either way, he's not looking for a long conversation, but neither are you.

You move past him into the main meeting room. A number of empty seats await toward the back. You quickly choose one and sit down. You're a little early, and the "service" or "gathering" or whatever they call it has not yet begun.

You take a few moments to cast your eyes about the room and take it all in. You observe the other people, whether they're in ties or shorts, whether they're old or young. You observe the furniture, the general décor, the platform or staging down front.

Maybe someone handed you a pamphlet or bulletin, so you leaf through its pages: design . . . church logo . . . announcements . . . list of programs . . . weekly schedule . . . a short message from the pastor, with a photo of him. You put the bulletin down and look around again.

Someone's playing music down front. If this is a traditional church, it might be an organ prelude. If it's a more contemporary church, it's a praise band rehearsing. You listen.

Throughout all of this, impressions are forming in your mind about this place and the kind of people who run it. Feelings are beginning to rise up. Is this place comfortable? Folksy? Austere? Hip?

It's right here, at this very moment, that I want to ask you a question: What's most important to you as you consider whether you will come back to this church? What is it that you *most want?*

Impatience and the Surface of Things

As a Christian and a first-time visitor, you've been observing the surface of things: how the room and people look, what the music sounds like. The trouble is, our fallen condition causes us to give an undue importance to what's on the surface, and Western culture accentuates those on-the-surface elements.

Many Christians, at this moment, may already know whether they will come back to this church. The service hasn't even begun, but they might have decided that it's too old or too young, too institutional or too irreverent.

And I'm sympathetic to the impulse. So many television commercials, so many interesting restaurants, so many store displays, so many movies, so many options over everything, and it's all too easy for me to be a critic of how things look or sound. And strange to say, it's even easy *to define* myself by the particular clothes I wear, the bands I listen to, or the movies I enjoy. Criticize my music and you criticize me.

Furthermore, we live in an instant society, and we've become impatient. We don't need to save money for a big purchase, we just swipe the credit card. We don't need libraries or encyclopedias; we have Internet search engines. We don't want to spend decades building a company with hard work; we want brilliant ideas, good marketing, and some media buzz.

Surely these things affect our expectations of Sunday morning and our approach to spirituality through the week.

The Patient Work of the Word

Yet here's what I want to plead with my fellow Christians: As you or I sit there wondering whether we'll come back to a church, the most important thing to consider is how seriously the church treats God's Word. Are the sermons meaty? Is the music theologically beefy? Do they read the Bible out loud? Do the public prayers reflect the priorities of the Bible?

As noted in chapters 2 and 3, what gives life to the dead and freedom to the slave is the Father's Word of the Son working through power of the Spirit. So you and I should primarily be looking for one thing when we gather with a church: God's Word.

Everything else that you set your eyes on when you walk into a church building is one of two things: either a platform for the Word or evidence of the Word's life-changing power, as I defined these two things in chapter 3. The building, the style of music, even the job of "greeter" is a platform (though the person and hopefully his heart attitude is much more— evidence of the Word's power!). As we decide what's important, we must remember that it's the Word alone that gives life and freedom.

Now, we should also ask whether there's evidence for belief in that Word. Have we found ourselves in a building full of theologically astute cold fish? Do the members care for one another and for the outsider? Do they have integrity? These are crucial questions. Still, sitting there in a weekly gathering, our ears should itch for the Word.

If they do, it probably means the fabric of our spirituality has been woven with threads of patience. Listening carefully is long, hard work. I don't know about you, but I find it much easier to spend two hours watching "the movie" than twenty hours reading "the book." Our globalized, fast-paced, media-intense world doesn't train us to sit quietly for long stretches of time and listen to one person talking. We're not accustomed to it, and we don't value it. Furthermore, television-commercial makers have learned how to pull our heart strings within thirty seconds. Do you want my attention? Then you need to engage my emotions—fast!

Yet Jesus compared the process of speaking God's Word to sowing seeds in the ground, and Isaiah compared it to the rain falling and giving life to the soil. Seeds yield their fruit *slowly*. Rain feeds a crop *slowly*. And so the Word works *slowly*. That's a tough pill for us today to swallow.

For instance, how long do you like your sermons to be? The author of Hebrews refers to his "word of exhortation" as being brief (13:22). It takes forty-five minutes to read Hebrews out loud. Does that seem like a brief sermon to you? As for a long sermon in the Bible, Paul once preached all night (Acts 20:7–11). How does that sound? Impossible? Perhaps, but most of us have watched movies into the wee hours.

When it comes to who we sleep with or how we spend our money, Christians know that our lives should look different than non-Christians. We recognize that these are morally significant matters. But I'd like to add something else to the list—something with even larger moral and spiritual consequences: how patient and diligent we are in listening to God's Word and, therefore, what we regard as important in our churches.

We must not prioritize the platform on which the Word speaks over the Word itself. The Word gathers the church, and so the church gathers for the Word. These are the two points I want to consider in the remainder of this chapter.

The Word Gathers the Church

In the last chapter, we saw that the Word sets us free as individuals. The electric current of Word and Spirit enters through our ears, jolts our hearts to a pulse, and bursts the iron shackles of sin. The Word saves us.

Yet its work doesn't stop there. It doesn't leave us as detached individuals. Rather, the Word gathers the church. Or, to say it the other way around, the church on earth is the fruit of the Word, just like a plant is the fruit of a seed that's been sown (see Mark 4:14).

The Word's electric, Spirit-filled vibrations reverberate outward and call a church into existence. It's like a magnet which causes a thousand individual shards of metal to gather and amass.

When I say the Word gathers the church, I don't mean it gathers "the universal church" in some abstract theological sense. No, I mean it gathers concrete groups of people, real assemblies. People arrive by foot. In come the sandals and sneakers, boots and loafers, heels and pumps, all walking through the door and onto one floor, or two if there's a balcony. All these individuals have been converted by the Word, and now the Word commands them not to neglect "to meet together" (Heb. 10:25).

Yet these individuals don't come together just because they are commanded. They come because they are citizens of the one whom they have confessed as Lord; and part of citizenship means gathering with other citizens to hear about the country they've not yet seen. They come because they are adopted sons and daughters, and children love to join the family at the dinner table for the meal of the Word. They come because they are sheep, and sheep belong in a herd that follows the Shepherd toward green pastures. They come because they are members of a body, and every part of the body needs every other part.

Pick whatever biblical metaphor for the church you want, the point is the same: a Christian's new DNA, which he's received from the Word and Spirit, knows that it now belongs to something larger. And he's not content to wait for that heavenly and end-time assembly. His new being longs to be gathered to other believers *now*—on earth. Like his new appetite to "put on" Christ's righteousness, so there's a new appetite to put on Christ's unity with God's people in a real assembly on earth.

The apostles maintained the same program—preach the Word.

This was one sign in my own life that I had truly been converted. When I was a nominal Christian, being around Christians was embarrassing to me. Then, somehow, I wanted to be around them. This desire began around the same time other new desires showed up, like the desire to read the Bible, fight sin, share the gospel, listen to sermons, and serve those around me. Looking back, I believe all of these were signs of a genuine conversion. The Word saved me, and then it gathered me to Christ's people—one more leaf raked onto the pile.

This is what we see in the New Testament again and again. People believe the Word and are saved, and then the Word either builds a church upon them (if there is none) or it adds them to a church. To begin with, we observe this pattern in the first church in Jerusalem:

- At Pentecost, Peter preached a sermon that culminated with the gospel words, "Repent and be baptized every one of you in the name of Jesus Christ for the forgiveness of your sins, and you will receive the *gift of the Holy Spirit.*" Then we read: "So those *who received his word* were baptized, and there were added that day about three thousand souls" (Acts 2:38, 41, all italics added).
- With a church so large, one might be tempted to try new strategies. But the apostles maintained the same program—preach the Word: "Many of those who had *heard the word* believed, and the number of the men came to about five thousand" (Acts 4:4).
- Then a moment of ethnic controversy hit the Jerusalem church. Still, the apostles resolved, "But we will devote ourselves *to prayer and to the ministry of the word*" (Acts 6:4). The result? "And *the word of God continued to increase,* and the number of the disciples multiplied greatly in Jerusalem" (Acts 6:7).

This pattern repeats itself throughout the book of Acts once the church in Jerusalem is scattered outward from persecution: "Those who were scattered preached the word wherever they went" (8:4 NIV). Several times we read a similar sounding refrain: "But the word of God increased and multiplied" (Acts 12:24); "The word of the Lord was spreading through the whole region" (13:49); "In this way the word of the Lord spread widely and grew in power" (19:20 NIV).[1] Now, Acts does not explicitly turn around and say, "And churches were built in all those places." But that's clearly the picture the author paints. Paul's second missionary journey, for instance, begins with the statement, "He went through Syria and Cilicia, strengthening the churches" (Acts 15:41). Which churches? The churches that were planted in those places where we had been told he preached the Word on his first journey. Throughout Acts, we watch as churches are established in Antioch, Philippi, Thessalonica, Rome, and elsewhere. The effect of the preached Word in a particular location is not just a bunch of individual Christians, but a church.

It's not surprising, then, that most of the New Testament epistles are written to *churches*, and the authors never really distinguish the beginning of their lives as Christians from the beginning of their lives as churches. In the following examples, every "you" and "your" is plural, and in every case the author ascribes the beginning of their life to the power of the Word or gospel:

- The church in Corinth: "Now I would remind you, brothers, of *the gospel I preached to you*, which you received, in which you stand, and by which you are being saved, if you hold fast to *the word I preached to you*" (1 Cor. 15:1–2, all italics added). The assumption is that their new lives as individual Christians and as a congregated assembly began when they embraced Paul's message. It's like a basketball coach writing to his whole team, "I remember when I first taught you to play basketball." By that he would be referring to when he taught them individually *and* as a team! The two are not to be separated.

- So with the church in Ephesus: "In him *you* also, when *you* heard the word of truth, the gospel of your salvation, and believed in him, were sealed with the promised Holy Spirit" (Eph. 1:13).
- Paul says similar things to the churches in Philippi, Colossae, and Thessalonica (Phil. 1:3, 5; Col. 1:5–6; see also 1 Thess. 1:5).
- And the same ideas are at least implied by the author of Hebrews (13:7), by James (1:21), by Peter (1 Peter 1:23, 25), by John (1 John 1:6, 10; 2:24), and by Jude (vv. 3, 20).

Again and again on the pages of Scripture, the Word converts people and adds them to local churches. It gathers the church. In light of such a uniform testimony, why would Christians show up on Sunday looking for anything else? Insofar as they do, their pastors should (1) teach them otherwise and (2) stop giving incentives.

The Church Gathers for the Word

In order to join my church, an individual must be interviewed by one of the elders. During the interview, the elder fills out a membership report form, which he afterward submits to all the elders. These reports are wonderfully heartening to read. Sometimes they describe remarkable adulthood conversions. Sometimes they tell the story of God's faithfulness since a person's childhood. But each one is a testimony of God's mercy, love, and power.

In just the last round of membership applications, several jumped out at me. One prospective member, who I'll call Tom, recalled his mother taking him to church occasionally as a child, but he got nothing out of it. When he married, Tom continued the pattern of attending church only once in a great while, this time for the sake of his daughter. About one year ago, he decided to attend our church as a Mother's Day gift for his mom. Tom came in the middle of a sermon series on 1 and 2 Samuel, and found the expositional preaching "jaw dropping." So he kept coming. At some point in the following months— Tom's not sure when—he was converted. He knew because he began reading the Bible on his own; began thinking about sin in a whole new way; began thinking about God's glory and name. I'd add that he also consistently began gathering with a church.

In the meantime, Tom's wife resisted attending because she didn't like leaving her children in the nursery. Jenny had never attended church as a child, and all the churches she had attended with her husband managed to avoid preaching the gospel. Still, she consented, began attending with Tom, heard the gospel, and has now repented and put her faith in Christ.

The elder who did their membership interviews said it was amazing to watch the couple interact. Something dramatic had happened only recently in both of their lives, and they were relating to each other in a whole new way.

In another membership report, Phillip (not his real name) described the experience of immigrating to the United States several years ago from an African nation. He had been converted in Africa, and so joined a church here in Washington that was comprised entirely of other individuals from his home nation. Phillip described it as a good church in many ways, and he and his wife profited spiritually from their time in this congregation. But at some point, they sensed that the church had become too enamored with maintaining its own ethnic distinctiveness. They knew they had to leave and find a place where the Word of the gospel was primary, not ethnic distinctiveness.

In some ways, these are ordinary Christian stories. I receive a batch of them every other month in preparation for our bi-monthly members meeting, and these three were in the last batch. I trust that other church leaders have similar stories of their own. But is not every Christian story an extraordinary example of God's love and power? In today's world, why would anyone in Washington, D.C., much less a young professional couple, show up in church? And then how would they get converted listening to sixty-minute sermons on the book of Samuel? Why would another couple, living in what for them is a foreign country, forsake the fellowship and love they share with their own countrymen, in order to find a church which emphasizes the words of a really old book?

God's people want to hear from God.

The answer to these questions, of course, is that the Word gathers the church, and then the church gathers to hear God's Word. God's people want to hear from God. A church's members should consist of those who have confessed Jesus as Lord. And so they gather to hear the Lord's words, to affirm their accountability to it, and to extend its ministry in one another's lives.

What should a church do, therefore, when it gathers? It should *make a house* for the Word. Paul writes, "Let the word of Christ dwell in you richly, teaching and admonishing one another in all wisdom, singing psalms and hymns and spiritual songs, with thankfulness in your hearts to God" (Col. 3:16). The word for "dwell," translated literally, means "make a house in." Paul then is telling us to let the Word of Christ come and make a house in our local churches through our teaching and singing. The Word should reverberate back and forth, from mouth to mouth and heart to heart. And a local church will be led astray when its weekly gatherings give primacy to anything other than the Word, from the Eucharist to programs for the poor.

With the Voice of Jesus

You *can* build a church around generational tastes in music and décor. Around an ethnicity. Around a choir program. Around a denominational identity. Around opportunities for young mothers, or a lively singles program, or even around the personality of a preacher. And often building your church around these things will produce immediate, visible results. It will require less patience.

Still, let me offer this alternative: We call out with the voice of Jesus. Remember, He promises that His sheep "will listen" to His voice (John 10:14, 16, 27; also 1 John 4:6).

Calling out with the voice of Jesus means the church's ministry of the Word must be primary and central, which is where we will turn for the remainder of this book—to preaching the Word, singing the Word, praying the Word, discipling the Word, and, once again, evangelizing with the Word.

For the next three chapters we will focus on the sermon. These chapters aren't just for the preaching pastor. They are relevant for every Christian for at least two reasons. First, every Christian is a *hearer* of God's Word. If you want to be a healthy eater, you need to learn what healthy food is. Don't just leave it to the cooks.

Second, every Christian is a *teacher* of God's Word. Jesus commanded every Christian to fulfill the Great Commission—to make disciples and teach them everything he has commanded (Matt. 28:19–20). And the author of Hebrews suggested that every Christian should be some kind of a teacher (Heb. 5:12). Mothers, how will you teach your children? Small group leaders, what will give true growth to your small groups? In the next three chapters, I'll be talking about preachers and sermons, but the principles are vital for all of us.

Note

1. For more on the power of the Word in the early church, see also Acts 8: 4, 14, 17; 10:44–45; 11:1; 14:13, 6–7, 21, 25; 15:35–36; 16:10, 13–14; 31–33; 17:2–4, 10–11, 23f; 18:1–5, 11; 19:1–6; 20:18–35; 28:23, 30–31).

Recommended Reading

Dever, Mark. *What Is a Healthy Church?* Wheaton, Ill.: Crossway, 2007.

Dever, Mark and Paul Alexander. *The Deliberate Church.* Wheaton, Ill.: Crossway, 2005.

Leeman, Jonathan. *The Church and the Surprising Offense of God's Love.* Wheaton, Ill.: Crossway, 2010.

PART 2

the
sermon

5 } the sermon exposes

We don't think your preaching will build this church. So we have decided not to nominate you as our next pastor." That is what the elders of a church said to me toward the end of a three-month interim pastorate.

It was a Sunday. We had just finished the church's evening service, which I had led. My wife had gone home. And the four elders and I were now sitting in the living room of the elder chairman. My wife and I had prayed that, God willing, the interim pastorate would turn into a full-time pastorate. Apparently, that was not going to happen.

What was wrong with my preaching? That was the obvious question. The four brothers focused their answer almost entirely on one thing: my faithfulness to the biblical text. They put it like this: "Your preaching has been fine from the standpoint of saying true things, and much of what you're saying comes out of the text you're preaching. The problem is, your sermons tend to be 20 to 30 degrees off the main point of the text."

The evaluation surprised me. I had *meant* to preach faithful biblical messages. That was my goal. I had the same philosophy of ministry as they. In the first few weeks of the interim pastorate, I had preached Psalms 1, 2, and 3. Then, I had turned to preaching my way through the book of Colossians, section by section. But 20 to 30 degrees off the main point of the text? Really?

Creative to a Fault

They pushed a little further. "Jonathan, we've known you for a few years, we love you, and we want to serve you, brother. So we've been asking ourselves how this could have happened. The main thing we have come up with is that you are very creative, and your creative impulse seems to show up almost every week. Half the time it works, and you say something in an interesting way. But half the time it doesn't work, and you miss the point of the text."

Hmmm, that hit home. I knew what they were talking about. In fact, I knew better than they did. Week after week I had labored to devise a fresh approach to the text. I could even remember saying to my wife, "These people have heard it all a hundred times. I need some new way to say it."

Here's an example. Our church was on the doorstep of a large state university, and we wanted to do a better job of reaching the university crowd. So I titled the Colossians series, "Philosophies of This World or Things Above," based on the theme of worldly philosophies in the book (see Col. 2:8). I used the error of a major philosopher to set up the biblical text for each week:

> *Week 1* on Colossians 1:1–14 was titled "Can Richard Rorty Know God's Will?"
> *Week 2* on 1:15–23 was called "What Kant (Be) Missed."
> *Week 3* on 1:24–2:5 was "Time, Hope, and Hegel."

You get the point. Even aside from the slightly pretentious nature of this enterprise, the more significant problem was that it allowed the philosophers to set the agenda. Instead of asking the very simple question, "What's the burden of this biblical text," I used the text to answer the challenge posed by the philosopher. Sometimes it worked. Sometimes it caused me to redirect the point of the text—I don't know—maybe 20 to 30 degrees.

Not only that, I knew that something else had been quietly transpiring in my heart over the prior months. I had grown restless with the desire to impress the congregation with my originality and spiritual insight. I wanted them to think I was a great preacher. And I wanted to impress these four men especially. As a result, the process of preparing "creative" sermons became stifling.

Strangely, how many preachers walk down this road? And how those four brothers blessed me by refusing to hire me! With gentle and loving words, they gave me a gift which, I trust, will serve my ministry for as long as the Lord gives me one. The embarrassment of failure and the prospect of unemployment made the lesson burn, but the Lord meant for the burn to sear the lesson onto my mind. Thinking back now, I can almost hear the hiss of a divine cow brand—"Just preach the point of the text!"—and thank God for it.

How Then Do We Preach?

Is it wrong then to use creativity in sermons? No. But I would say we should be very careful with creativity. After all, what builds the church—our creative ideas or God's Word? The answer is the same in every time and every place: God's Word working by God's Spirit.

Yet, hold on—is it that simple? We concluded chapter 2 by observing that God speaks through human preachers and human words, which raises the matter of our involvement. Jesus prayed for "those who will believe in me through *their word*" (John 17:20), which sounds like we're to do something more than standing up and reading the red-letter words from a red-letter Bible. It sounds like we're to craft our own sentences and paragraphs, our own outlines and illustrations. But if that's the case, how can "our words" be "His Word"?

Maybe this question hasn't troubled you, but it has perplexed me for years. I can accept the theological proposition that God's Word alone gives life to God's people. It's exciting! But what does that mean for what we're supposed to do beyond reading the actual text of the Bible? How do we proclaim *God's Word* versus *proclaim human ideas* when we are the ones writing the sermon or teaching the lesson?

That's the main question of this chapter: How do we most faithfully proclaim God's Word, such that His Spirit will work mightily?

The Goal: Plainly Exposing God's Word

The question may have perplexed me on and off for years, but finally I think the answer is quite simple: God speaks through us whenever we plainly and modestly relate whatever He has already said in the Bible. Preachers are to expose God's message, simply and directly.

For instance, this is what the Levites did for the Israelites in Nehemiah's time: "They read from the Book of the Law of God, making it clear and giving the meaning so that the people could understand what was being read" (Neh. 8:8 NIV). They read it, and they explained it. They faithfully transmitted its message. That's all.

The transaction that should occur in preaching is simple because it's an everyday transaction.

- A mailman doesn't deliver his own letters, but someone else's.
- A reporter doesn't make up the news, but reports it.
- A receptionist doesn't receive a phone call, and then make up a phone message; she passes on the caller's message.

Likewise, a human preacher preaches God's Word not when he communicates his own message or ideas, but God's. D. A. Carson calls this "re-revelation." God has revealed a message in the past through an apostle or prophet. And now He uses a preacher to reveal not a new message but that same message once more. When that happens, the congregation may be listening to a preacher speak, but they're hearing from God. Call it "re-revelation" if you want, or call it delivering the mail, reporting the news, or passing on the message.

Our bigger-than-life-or-death goal as preachers must be to expose God's Word. Expose what He says.

Now, there are more factors involved in preaching, because

as preachers we're speaking through our personalities and through our cultural conditioning. Plus, we're interested in addressing the particular concerns and challenges of our particular people. Still, we must not let these realities cause us to take our eyes off the ball. It is God's Word and our faithfulness to it that give life, not something that our personalities or experiences can *contribute* to God's Word. Nowhere does the Bible say that our creativity will build God's church. How arrogant (and burdensome) to think it might!

Therefore, our bigger-than-life-or-death goal as preachers must be to expose God's Word. Expose what He says. Expose His message.

Now, if a mature and wise man is able to harness creativity, colorful illustrations, contextual sensitivity, and even his charismatic personality as servants that aid the process of exposing God's Word, fine. But in my experience, creative people don't need to focus on being creative, and charismatic people don't need to focus on being charismatic. Nor do relational people need to focus on being relational. They talk, and it happens. And, in my experience, focusing on the charisma or creativity, ironically, distracts you from the message and often ends up distorting it. But even if someone wants to push back and observe that everyone can work on becoming a better communicator, which I happily concede, I still want to keep this one fact squarely in front of our eyes: The preacher gives his hearers a chance at life *only insofar as he succeeds in faithfully reproducing what God has already said.* So focus on that!

Perhaps I can illustrate the point—creatively?!—by stepping into a different domain. Suppose that a creative, charismatic, or relational person works as a press secretary for a U.S. senator, as several members of my church do. The senator asks his press secretary to explain his position on health care in his absence at a press conference. What's the secretary's goal? To explain the senator's position clearly. That's it. Now, with time and practice, a good secretary might learn to pepper his or her explanations with a little creativity or charisma in order to make the message clearer or lower the defenses of his or her audience. But no sensible secretary would ever think of letting such qualities get in the way of a pristine and faithful presentation of the senator's message. That's the only goal. Otherwise, he or she will be fired.

Preachers, too, can be encouraged to employ creativity, charisma, or any other such device, but such devices must remain lowly workers, unassuming eunuchs who usher palace visitors toward the royal throne of God's Word, always serving the message and never mastering it. The plain and bare goal of preaching is to expose God's Word, and everything in the preacher's arsenal must unite toward that one end.

The Best Manner of Preaching: Expositional

If one agrees with the discussion so far, it shouldn't be too difficult to take the next step. I propose that the best—yes, I mean "best"—manner of preaching is preaching that, quite simply, *exposes* God's Word. Indeed, we could even coin a phrase that describes preaching which exposes God's Word. How about *expositional?* And the sole distinctive of expositional preaching, we could say, is that it faithfully exposes God's text.

Of course I'm not making up the term "expositional." But I do mean to remove any misconceptions you might have, and so I want to try defining it from scratch. First, remove anything about the personality of the preacher. Preachers charismatic and preachers calm are gladly admitted into this league. Second, get rid of anything about the length of the biblical text, as if to say expositional sermons cover only a verse or two. They can cover as much or as little as you determine. Third, forget for a moment all the other incidentals such as the presence or absence of humor, creativity, or good stories. Prudence may offer counsel on these matters, but none of these things is definitive. Last, but not least, please don't assume that expositional preaching aims just at the head, but not the heart, soul, or will. Bad expositional preaching might, that's true, but every kind of preaching can be done poorly.

One thing is definitive for an expositional sermon: It lays out the meaning and purpose of a biblical text clearly. It says, "Here is the point of this text, and it's relevant to you, no matter who you are, where you are from, or what's happening in your life right now." The preacher concentrates all his powers on reproducing the burden of the Bible in the hearts and minds of the people, and he avoids letting anything in his person get in the way of that goal. He'd rather risk boring or offending his congregation than depriving them of the opportunity to hear what God says. As we saw, he knows that he gives his hearers a chance at true life only insofar as he succeeds in faithfully reproducing what God has already said.

The sermon event is not just an information transfer. . . It's God's action of personally engaging the hearers.

The cleanest definition of an expositional sermon that I've seen is Mark Dever's: An expositional sermon is a sermon in which *the point of a biblical text is the point of the sermon, applied to the life of the congregation.* And to speak of "the point" of the text, I would add, we need to consider both the text's content and its purpose. Does the text call its hearers to self-examination and confession? To repentance? To holy living? To praise? To wonder and joy? So should the sermon. The sermon event is not just an information transfer—"This text says that Jesus is God." It's God's action of personally engaging the hearers—"This text says that Jesus is God. And right now, through my very words, you're hearing Him call you to bow before Him." The preacher's words are God's words to the extent they are faithful to the content and purpose of God's words. As Peter puts it, "If anyone speaks, he should do it as one speaking the very words of God" (1 Peter 4:11 NIV).

In my opinion, therefore, preaching the point of the text in a way that's faithful to both content and purpose means being sensitive to literary genre, and potentially adapting one's style. A plain three-point sermon might be appropriate for an epistle. But something is lost when the same style is applied to a powerful narrative like Joseph's, or Esther's, or Jesus' resurrection. Why do children love to hear the story of Daniel and the lion's den? Because in a narrative, the setting, the tone, the interplay of developing characters, and the surprise and delight of a plot's resolution give power to a text, even theological power. Faithfulness to that particular text, I believe, requires articulating the propositional lessons of this story; but it also requires *moving* the hearer through the action of the story, step by step, so that the hearer can experience a childlike wonder and awe at the power and faithfulness of God. In short, narrative might require something slightly different than epistle, just as poetry should be different than law, and wisdom need be different than apocalyptic.

Yet in every genre, the preacher's goal is the same: laying the burden or point of the text upon the congregation.

What about Other Kinds of Preaching?

Does this mean that other kinds of preaching are wrong? Not necessarily, and there is a time and place for other kinds of preaching. Let me mention just two.

Topical Preaching

For instance, a pastor might decide that his congregation needs to spend concentrated time meditating on the family, on the church, or on some other topic of seemingly acute relevance. Let me offer three thoughts about determining one's weekly preaching schedule by topic.

First, the preacher serves his congregation, as we've been saying, only insofar as he succeeds in faithfully reproducing what God has already said. So even if he's not taking his sermon from one particular text, the sermon will still have life changing power only to the extent that it does faithfully teach what the Bible says. Again, God gives life through His Word, not through human ideas.

Second, topical preaching lives in the continual risk of offering something half-as-powerful as expositional preaching because its primary focus is seldom on the full burden of any one text, but on an idea preselected by the preacher. Such sermons almost always employ biblical texts, and they will often say true things from those texts. But too often they fail to preach any given text in its fullness because the preacher comes to the text with an agenda.

For instance, suppose a preacher wants to preach a series on prayer. One week, he employs Hebrews 4:16, which talks about drawing near the throne of grace with confidence, and the main point of his sermon is "We should always pray with confidence!" Is this preacher plainly *exposing* this text with all its divinely intended life-giving power? Well, Hebrews 4:16 is about the fact that, because the sinless Christ offered a more perfect sacrifice than the Levitical priests, God's wrath against us has been removed and we can draw near to him in a reconciled relationship. One application of this fact is that we can confidently draw near God in prayer. But principally the text is a meditation on the gospel itself. Can't preachers say all this when discussing prayer? Sure, but often they won't.

When the preacher begins with the topic and then goes in search of texts on that topic, his approach to the text will be *shaped by* and probably *limited to* the question that he asks of the text. In this series on prayer, he's approaching the text and asking, "What does this verse have to say about prayer?" He is not asking, "What's the point of this text?"

This brings me to a third point about topical preaching. The Bible knows what's relevant to every congregation far better than the greatest of pastors. It knows what a congregation needs more than the congregation knows. And frankly, in our fallenness and finitude, none of us would pick a good number of the topics or themes in the Bible. Preachers sometimes say that a good preacher will exegete both the Bible and his hearers. It's very true that knowing one's audience strengthens one's preaching. Before preaching in my own church, I often turn slowly and prayerfully through the pages of our church directory. Seeing the pictures of their faces calls to mind their particular trials, temptations, and evidences of grace. It helps me to focus the meaningfulness of the text on *them*. At the same time, Australian pastor Phillip Jensen is surely right to say that the Word of God can exegete our people far better than we can. It can unpack and explain them. It knows what they really need.

In a topical series, however, God and His all-wise Word does not set the agenda for what the congregation learns. Too often it's set by the preacher's wisdom, his likes and dislikes, his hobbyhorses, the areas in which he feels competent, and his limitations. But when a preacher preaches straight through a book of the Bible, God sets the agenda. And the preacher learns along with the congregation.

I would sum all of this up by saying that topical sermons

may be helpful from time to time, not as the rule. The regular diet of a church should consist of sermon series that move straight through books of the Bible, whether in big or little chunks. Why is that? Presenting expository sermons book by book:

- allows God and God's wisdom to set the agenda, not the preacher's wisdom;
- prevents preachers from indulging their hobbyhorses;
- allows the preacher to learn along with the congregation, rather than limiting the congregation to what the preacher already knows;
- requires a preacher and a congregation to learn about God as God has revealed Himself, not as they want Him to be revealed; and
- requires a preacher to preach the easy bits and the difficult bits of the Bible.

Dialogical Preaching

A number of writers have been promoting dialogical preaching lately. Such preaching focuses on the back and forth nature of dialogue, but places this conversation into the preaching event. It's said to be particularly appropriate in these postmodern days since no one believes anymore that "one man has all the answers." Dialogues give every member of the community an opportunity to express himself or herself and offer a perspective on God's Word. Or it's said to be sufficient for those Christians who don't attend churches at all, but pursue growing as Christians through dialoging with other Christians privately.

No doubt, group conversations about God's Word, as in inductive Bible studies, can be rich and sweet. It is encouraging to hear the young and old, mature and immature, testify to their experience of God's grace through the biblical text being discussed.

At the same time, God has gifted some—not all—to be pastors and teachers and given them as gifts to His church (Eph. 4:7–13). And He means to particularly bless and grow His church through them.

The pattern throughout Scripture is for a man—a judge, a prophet, an apostle, a preacher— to speak authoritatively on behalf of God: "Thus says the Lord . . ." The speaker's authority does not derive from himself; it derives from the Word. It's tied to his faithful presentation of it. The congregation, on the other hand, learns what it

> *The goal isn't to exchange perspectives, but to hear what God says.*

means to submit to God by submitting to His authoritative Word as it's preached. The goal isn't to exchange perspectives, but to hear what God says. Every Christian (including the preacher) must understand that first and foremost we live *under* God's authoritative Word. This reality is best demonstrated and practiced through the preaching event, a place where we learn to sit quietly and listen. The preacher, if he has been faithful, has been sitting quietly and listening all week!

Just Passing on the King's Mail

I don't know if I would ever choose to preach about divorce. But when you're preaching through Mark's gospel, you don't have much choice. Finish preaching chapter 9, and there it is at the top of chapter 10, staring up at you like the lidless eye of a dead fish.

And here I was, midway through another interim pastorate, this time preaching through the Gospel of Mark. Prior to my coming, the church had never once—the elders told me—gone straight through a book of the Bible. Yet people were generally responding well. Everyone was even a little surprised, I think, that Mark turned out to be so relevant and encouraging to their lives.

One of the things that excited me most was to watch the congregation begin approaching the Sunday morning gatherings differently. As we finished up Mark 9, I guess quite a few people noticed the Bible's subheading—"Divorce" or "Teaching about Divorce"—because a number of people were asking about it the following week. Nobody had ever preached on divorce, the elders told me. The church was learning to anticipate hearing from God.

So the following Sunday, I told them what God says: "Divorce is sin, which means some of you need to repent." I received one letter that week from a person declaring that the church was not for her. But I also had one middle-aged woman who was about to consent to her husband's request for a divorce approach me later in the week and say, "Tell me more." And right after the sermon, a thirty-year-old man came up to me and said, "I only became a Christian a few months ago, and now I want to marry the woman who led me to the Lord, but I'm divorced. What do I do? Can we have lunch?"

Tough questions, to be sure, but wonderfully these people were turning to God's Word in a way they had not before. They were turning to God! What was my involvement? All I did was deliver the king's mail: "Here you go. Here's what the king says." And then the Spirit began doing the real work!

Recommended Reading

Ash, Christopher. *The Priority of Preaching.* Ross-Shire, Scotland: Christian Focus Publications, 2009.

Bridges, Charles. *Christian Ministry.* Carlisle, Pa.: The Banner of Truth Trust, 1997. First published in 1830.

Ryken, Leland and Todd Wilson, eds. *Preach the Word: Essays on Expository Preaching.* Wheaton, Ill.: Crossway, 2007.

Stott, John. *Between Two Worlds: The Art of Preaching in the Twentieth Century.* Grand Rapids: Eerdmans, 1982.

6 } the sermon announces

A group of American Christians in the nineteenth century planned to visit London for a week. Their friends, excited for the opportunity, encouraged them to go hear two of London's famous preachers and bring back a report.

On Sunday morning after their arrival, the Americans attended Joseph Parker's church. They discovered that his reputation for eloquent oratory was well deserved. One exclaimed after the service, "I do declare, it must be said, for there is no doubt, that Joseph Parker is the greatest preacher that ever there was!"

The group wanted to return in the evening to hear Parker again, but they remembered that their friends would ask them about another preacher named Charles Spurgeon.

So on Sunday evening they attended the Metropolitan Tabernacle, where Spurgeon was preaching. The group was not prepared for what they heard, and as they departed, one of them again spoke up, "I do declare, it must be said, for there is no doubt, that Jesus Christ is the greatest Savior that ever there was!"

I recently heard this story from Richard Phillips. He heard it from his seminary professor. Whether it actually happened or is a piece of folklore that has grown up around Spurgeon, known as "the Prince of Preachers," I'm not sure. What is sure, however, is that this is the response Christian preachers want to produce in their congregations—a reveling in Jesus Christ. And this is the response, I hope, that Christians want to have Sunday after Sunday.

Christian preaching, if it's about anything, is about *announcing* the amazingly good news of Jesus Christ.

Announcing and Confronting

In chapter 5, I argued that right preaching exposes God's Word, which is sort of like saying that an actor should play the part of his character. But now let's think a bit more about the character itself, the Bible. The Bible does two things: It *announces* what God has done, and it *confronts* its hearers with this news and its implications. For a preacher to expose the Bible, therefore, he must expose the Bible's announcement and confrontation. More to the point, he must, like the actor, play the part of announcer and confronter.

For instance, Jesus walks onto stage in Mark's gospel, proclaiming,

Announcement → "The kingdom of God is at hand;

Confrontation →	Repent and believe in the gospel!" (Mark 1:15).

The preacher, in order to faithfully expose or "re-reveal" a text like this one, should follow this same pattern. He might say something like the following:

Announcement →	"Friends, Jesus came to establish His rule in our lives through His life, death, and resurrection."
Confrontation →	"We are now called to turn away from our sinful self-rule and put our trust in Him. He calls us to do this today!"

These sermonic words involve more than an information transfer, like one hears in a college classroom. They expose the pertinent information, yes, but they also expose the hearer to the same announcement and confrontation: "Hey, this applies to you!" To borrow a word from Darrell Johnson, the preacher "participates" in the text's purposes by personally engaging the listener with those purposes.[1]

The pattern of Mark 1:15 characterizes the whole Bible, and, therefore, this pattern must characterize all preaching and teaching of the Bible. Throughout *Reverberation* I've said that the Word gives life to the church. Now I need to specify what the Word is, particularly in relation to the gospel. It's in the gospel that we see both the announcement and confrontation most pointedly. This chapter will focus on the announcement, and chapter 7 on the confrontation. Understanding these matters, again, is relevant not only for preachers, but for anyone who wants to encounter God through His Word as a hearer and as a teacher. And that should be all of us.

What Is the Word?

Every profession has a way of separating the good from the bad. In the world of magazine journalism, where I once worked, one test of every article or opinion piece is whether it offers something *new*.

If you have ever run in preachers' circles—not the most glamorous of circles, to be sure—you would know that preachers, too, have a number of standard ways of separating good sermons from bad. One helpful test is to ask whether a man's sermon could have been preached by a Jewish rabbi or a Muslim imam. This question is not meant to disparage rabbis or imams. It's simply a way of acknowledging that there should be something distinctively Christian about a Christian sermon; namely, it should point to the person and work of Christ. Suppose, for instance, that a Sunday morning sermon focuses on the Fifth Commandment, and the preacher emphasizes the different ways to honor your parents, but says nothing about Christ. You would be justified in saying that a rabbi or an imam could have preached that sermon, and in wondering whether it was a truly *Christian* sermon.

Recently, I discovered a new test that can be used to separate good Christian teaching from bad: Can the teaching be adopted and heralded by a Mexican drug cartel? According to a Mexican government intelligence report obtained by the magazine *Milenio Semanal* (May 30, 2009), it turns out that one American evangelical's best-selling book is required reading for every member of the criminal gang known as *La Familia*. Apparently, the boss and spiritual leader of the gang, who is known as *El Más Loco* or The Craziest One, has become obsessed with this writer's affirmations that "God designed men to be dangerous" and that every man must have "a battle to fight . . . an adventure to live." When the crazy one is not overseeing the marijuana and cocaine traffic between Columbia, Mexico, the United States, and Europe or decapitating members of local police forces, he is hiring rural teachers to spread these ideas throughout the Mexican countryside.

I have not read this writer's books. But I wonder whether his moral exhortations to a wild and godly manliness are rooted in the foolish gospel of a crucified king. Clearly, *El Más Loco* doesn't stumble over the message; he proclaims it.

All of this raises the question: What is the "Word" that Christian preachers (and writers) are supposed to preach?

Suppose I am preaching about Samson from the book of Judges. If there was ever a man with "an adventure to live," it was Samson. Will observing such virtues about every Sunday school boy's favorite red-blooded judge cause the Spirit to move in power by giving life to the spiritually dead? Peter tells his readers that they had been "born again . . . through the living and abiding word of God." Could it have been stories of Samson's escapades that did the trick? Certainly Judges is a part of God's Word.

All sixty-six books proclaim one basic message. . . "The Christ will suffer and rise from the dead."

I think the answer to this last question is, It depends. If Samson had been preached *properly*, then, yes. But rightly preaching Judges takes more than extolling Samson's virile virtues with a chest-thumping call to masculinity. To preach Samson rightly, one must explain Judges 14 to 16 in their own context, and then one must explain how those chapters relate to the message of the entire Bible. One must preach a *Christian* sermon by demonstrating how the story of Samson leads us to Jesus Christ.

The basic insight here is that the sixty-six books of the Bible, written over thousands of years by dozens of authors in Hebrew, Aramaic, and Greek, have one divine author. And that one divine author takes all sixty-six books to proclaim one basic message. I could explain that one message to you by reading the hundreds of thousands of words that constitute those sixty-six books. Or I can explain that one message to you with thirty-one words spoken by Jesus: "The Christ will suffer and rise from the dead on the third day, and repentance and forgiveness of sins will be preached in his name to all nations, beginning at Jerusalem" (Luke 24:46–47 NIV).

Are these words really a summary of the Bible's message? Jesus seems to say as much. Here's the context of these thirty-one words:

> *[Jesus] said to them, "This is what I told you while I was still with you: Everything must be fulfilled that is written about me in the Law of Moses, the Prophets and the Psalms." Then he opened their minds so they could understand the Scriptures. He told them, "This is what is written: The Christ will suffer and rise from the dead on the third day."* (Luke 24:44–46 NIV)

Notice Jesus' words "This is what is written," referring to the entire Old Testament (Law, Prophets, and Writings, or "Psalms" for short). The words that follow—"The Christ will suffer . . ."—don't appear to be written in the Old Testament, but He "opened their minds" to see that this indeed is the message of the entire Old Testament. It's summed up in the thirty-one words. Here, Luke is summing up the message of his book, as well as the New Testament Gospels as a whole. And the New

Testament Epistles, too, are fundamentally centered on this message and its implications for our lives. As Paul puts it, "For I delivered to you as of first importance what I also received: that Christ died for our sins in accordance with the Scriptures, that he was buried, that he was raised on the third day in accordance with the Scriptures" (1 Cor. 15:3–4; see also Acts 3:18, 21, 24; 17:2, 3; 26:22, 23; 1 Peter 1:11).

In other words, the news announced in the sixty-six books of the Bible is summarized in what the New Testament writers call the "good news" or the "gospel." It's almost like comparing the headline of a news story and the story itself. The newspaper headline "Yankees Win World Series!" captures the basic message, while the news story that follows provides all the details of the game. If you have read that four-word headline and nothing more, you can say you have heard the "news" because you know the basic point—the Yankees won. The whole article is the "news"; and the headline is the "news."

In a similar way, all sixty-six books of the Bible constitute God's "Word"; and the few words of the gospel message constitute the "Word." This is why we so often see New Testament writers using the word "gospel" interchangeably with "word" (e.g. 1 Cor. 15:1–2; 1 Peter 1:23, 25).

Expositional Preaching
Must Be Gospel-Focused

What this means is that expositional preaching and teaching will always be gospel-focused. No matter what part of Scripture you mean to expose, the gospel should eventually come into view. Failing to do so means that you may well be distorting whatever text you mean to expose.

Let me explain the point this way. Suppose you did *not* read either the headline or the entire article about the Yankees' victory. But you did read one paragraph in the middle of the article about the Yankees relief pitcher entering the game in the seventh inning. Suppose further that a friend called you and asked if you had heard the "news" about the game, and you said, "Yes, the Yankees relief pitcher replaced the starter in the seventh inning!" He'd probably stop calling you to talk baseball. It's not that the seventh inning relief pitcher is unimportant; it's just that its importance depends entirely on how it affected the outcome of the game.

Reading only one paragraph in a news story is like making a big deal about Samson's amazing feats and saying nothing more. It's an interesting detail, but it's only one detail in one subplot of a much grander story. And its significance depends entirely on how it contributes to this larger story. Failing to locate it within the larger story, therefore, distorts its meaning, because it turns it into something significant in and of itself.

The story of the whole Bible, remember, is about Jesus Christ, and if the Bible had a headline, it might be something like, "Jesus Wins!" So whatever we might want to say about Samson's strength, we must explain how the particular details of Judges 14 to 16 contribute to the game that Jesus eventually wins if we mean to expose it faithfully.

How does it contribute? How could a preacher properly write the paragraph about Samson in the news story that is headlined with the words, "Jesus Wins"? There are a number of ways. Here are three. First, you could take the *typological* route by talking about Samson as a type of Christ. You would say that he is a God-anointed judge, endued with remarkable power through the Holy Spirit, who is handed over to the enemies of God's people for the purpose of rescuing God's people (e.g. Judg. 15:14–15; 16:30). Some might dispute whether Samson is really a type of Christ, and suggest instead that he merely presents an analogy. We certainly need to be careful about drawing such connections too quickly lest we allegorize Scripture. Still, the larger point here is to recognize that God often works in repeated patterns—types, analogies, symbols, and so on—so that the earlier occurrences of a pattern help us to interpret the occurrence of the same pattern in Christ, taking note of both similarities and differences.

Second, you could take the *thematic* route to get from Samson to Christ, a point I learned from a Tim Keller lecture. The scriptural canon is held together by a number of themes that come to the surface every so often, like a thread in a piece of cloth which appears, disappears, and appears again. The goal here would be to ask what threads appear in this book and then to trace those threads all the way to Christ. A few threads that might be worth following include Israel's unwillingness to follow the Lord (every man doing as he pleased); questions about intermarrying with the nations (as Samson does); God's covenant faithfulness (giving them judge after judge); and the inability of every judge to be the perfect deliverer (thereby exposing a deeper need than rescue from the Philistines).

Third, one could take the *systematic theology* route. What does Samson teach us about humankind—both our strengths and weaknesses? What does Samson's story teach us about God—His patience with His people and His determination to judge sin? What does his story teach us about our need for a Savior—for one who will not disappoint us like every judge or king who has ever lived, except one?

Samson's strength is striking. He fells a thousand Philistines with the jawbone of a donkey. But how much more striking is the picture of Christ coming on the last day, with a sword coming out of His mouth with which to strike down the nations, treading the winepress of the fury of the wrath of God Almighty (Rev. 19:15)! Only this judge is perfectly just and good.

Samson's death is also striking. He defeats his enemies and

rescues God's people through his death. Then again, Samson's folly and pride led to his death. Not so with Jesus, who deliberately went to His death in humility. Samson should indeed provoke our wonder—but our wonder at Christ, not Samson.

In short, an expositional sermon on Judges 14 to 16 should be a gospel sermon, not a sermon that could be preached in a synagogue or a mosque. And the same is true of any sermon from the Bible. No matter where a text is located on the plotline, it should always be preached with the entire plotline in view. Those who argue or preach otherwise may have well-developed eyes for Scripture's rich diversity, but they have lost sight of its glorious unity. Interpreting the Bible requires us to not only ask why the human author included a particular story or statement, we must also ask why the divine author included that story or statement in the Bible.

We're interested in announcing what God has done or promised to do.

Expositional Preaching Announces

In all of this, we're interested in announcing what God has done or promised to do. Right Christian preaching should always include the proclamation of what God has done in creation and redemption. He has created. He has given His law. He has condemned. He has sent His Son. He has prepared the way of salvation. He is now gathering His church, whom He will eventually rescue entirely. He will judge. Thus He has spoken.

Many Christian churches fail right here Sunday after Sunday. Sermons and small group lessons focus on "steps to a healthy marriage" and "ways to battle doubt" and "how to care for the community" and "walking like Jesus walked." Yet teachers fail to place these good ideas within the context of God's promised and fulfilled work.

When Christians preach, every command, every exhortation, every "how to" must be grounded in the gospel. Take the command not to steal. A rabbi or an imam can preach the biblical command not to steal, and they can apply this command to different areas of life: "God says not to steal. So don't steal from your neighbors. Don't steal from your boss." But this is not a Christian sermon precisely because it's not grounded in the announcement of what God has done.

Exhorting Christians means re-announcing that Christ has purchased them out of stealing through His death and resurrection. Any confrontation must be grounded in Christ's accomplished work.

The same goes for exhorting non-Christians. One must begin by announcing the holiness of God; God's command not to steal; and the sad reality that we have all stolen. One must then announce the good news that Jesus lived a perfect life and didn't steal, but died on the cross for thieves like us. Only after all that the confrontation comes: "Turn away from your stealing, and put your trust in Christ."

The Problem with Self-Help Teaching

In Christian teaching, any and all challenges must be placed within the context of announcing what God has done or promises to do. It's the very opposite of self-help teaching.

I admit it's easy to jump straight to the "should dos," "to dos," and "how tos" when preaching or teaching. It seems to meet the listeners where they are. It has the "appearance of wisdom" (Col. 2:23). It feels practical, applicable, and responsible. Yet, in the process, evangelical churches and books become filled with moralism.

In my experience, many evangelical churches proclaim the gospel as the path of salvation, but then quickly switch to moralism and self-help as the way of sanctification. Week after week, they offer motivational therapy. When such moralistic or motivational preaching abounds, Christians become nice and well-meaning. They tell their children to be good and to do good. Maybe they tithe. They often sincerely believe the gospel. And we should praise God for granting such fruit. But we should be jealous for more, since people's faith often remains shallow, ineffective, and anonymous in such churches. Most members don't build their lives around encouraging one another in the faith. They show up for an hour or two on Sunday, and then go home. They don't reorient their weekly schedules and budgets around discipleship, evangelism, hospitality, or caring for others.

Gospel Preaching vs. Motivational Preaching

Moralistic or motivational preaching seems wise because it appeals to a person's natural desires—desires for growth, change, love, being better. Everyone wants these things, Christian or not. But moralistic or motivational preaching can only motivate a person so far—as far as one's internal resources can take a person. "Do you want these things? Then grab them!" Everything depends on how much energy I have to grab the better life.

Gospel preaching, on the other hand, sounds foolish at first blush. It points to God on the cross, to which the natural response, at best, is, "Fascinating story, but what does that have to do with me?" Still, gospel preaching resolves to keep saying the same thing over and over, coming at the subject from as many angles as there are texts and subplots in the Scriptures. Amazingly, it disdains "eloquent words of wisdom," and it does so "lest the cross of Christ be emptied of its power" (1 Cor. 1:17). Sure enough, the preaching comes "in demonstration of the Spirit and of power" (1 Cor. 2:4). It gives hearers faith to believe that real change can come from the all-powerful God who raised Jesus from the dead. They hear of these mighty acts and discover that they, too, can cast themselves on this mighty and merciful God. Then, as faith increases, they discover that they can do all things through Christ.

If motivational preaching can motivate a person only as far as the flesh goes, gospel preaching motivates a person as far as God goes. After all, it doesn't just motivate, it transforms. It creates anew.

Worldly wisdom will always tempt us to motivate people with commands and how-tos. Godly wisdom knows there is a time and place for commands and confrontation. But it recognizes the Holy Spirit-charged power of the announcement, the message, the good news. Kevin DeYoung has put it well: "The secret of the gospel is that we actually do more when we hear less about all we need to do for God and hear more about all that God has already done for us."[2]

One Gospel-Charged Church

I recently read a report about one remarkable church-planting team. They relied entirely on the power of the gospel to plant a church in a city where no Christian witness existed. Like many teams, they received a little bit of financial support from a sending church, but they also had to support themselves with daily work. Certainly no money was available for flashy signs, flyers, Vacation Bible School supplies, a music band, a medical clinic, or anything else that might attract attention. So they contented themselves with finding one of the local "watering holes"—as a missionary friend of mine puts it—and preaching the gospel to whomever would listen.

Interestingly, they devoted themselves to preaching the gospel exclusively from the Old Testament. A large number of people responded positively. Many conversions occurred. This in turn provoked jealous opposition from another local religious group, who involved the city's officials. Eventually that led to the team's eviction from the city. All told, the church planting team had only a month (maybe a little longer) to preach before they were evicted.

But the story continued. In spite of the planters' premature departure, the church prospered and grew. Their persecutors continued to persecute, but the church responded with joy. Occasional questions did arise for the young believers on several doctrinal issues, but the church's works of faith and labors of love began to be noticed across their region. The gospel even spread beyond their country due to their witness and work.

What accounted for their remarkable change and growth, even in the face of persecution? Here's the answer the lead planter gave: "Our gospel came to [them] not only in word, but also in power and in the Holy Spirit and with full conviction." What's more, he said, they "received the word in much affliction, with the joy of the Holy Spirit."

Of course, these are Paul's words to the church in Thessalonica (1 Thess. 1:5–6). It's a truly remarkable story. An unreached city. Several planters. No church building. No outreach programs. Just the Old Testament. A great many conversions across ethnic lines. Gospel unity. The onset of persecution. Perseverance. Growth. Witness. An international reputation. You can read about it in Acts 17 and in the letters themselves.

Behind the remarkable story, says Paul, are words—words backed up by the power of the Holy Spirit to produce conviction, joy, and obedience. And it all began with an announcement: "This Jesus, whom I proclaim to you, is the Christ" (Acts 17:3).

Is it possible that a small team of planters could walk into one of the global metropolises of today in the West or East armed only with the Bible? Could they preach Christ crucified and watch a church grow up out of nothing, even in the face of opposition?

Notes

1. Darrell W. Johnson, *The Glory of Preaching: Participating in God's Transformation of the World* (Downers Grove, Ill.: InterVarsity, 2009).
2. Kevin DeYoung, "On Mission, Changing the World, and Not Being Able To Do It All," http://thegospelcoalition.org/blogs/kevindeyoung/2009/08/25/on-mission-changing-world-and-not-being/.

Recommended Reading

Chapell, Bryan. *Christ Centered Preaching.* Grand Rapids: Baker, 1994.

Clowney, Edmund. *Preaching and Biblical Theology.* Phillipsburg, N.J.: P&R, 2002. First published in 1961.

Dempster, Stephen. *Dominion and Dynasty.* Ed. D. A. Carson. Downers Grove, Ill.: InterVarsity, 2003.

Gilbert, Greg. *What Is the Gospel?* Wheaton, Ill.: Crossway, 2010.

Lawrence, Michael. *Biblical Theology in the Life of the Church,* Wheaton, Ill.: Crossway, 2010.

Dictionary of Biblical Theology. Ed. Rosner, Brian, T. Desmond Alexander, Graeme Goldsworthy and D. A. Carson. Downers Grove, Ill.: InterVarsity, 2000.

Anything by Graeme Goldsworthy, such as *According to Plan* (Downers Grove, Ill.: InterVarsity, 1991), *Preaching the Whole Bible as Christian Scripture* (Grand Rapids: Eerdmans, 2000), or *Gospel-Centered Hermeneutics* (Downers Grove, Ill.: InterVarsity, 2006).

7 } the sermon confronts

The preacher's text for the morning came from the book of Joshua. I don't remember which one, but the passage included one of those verses on the Bible's "difficult to stomach" list, something about God commanding Joshua to enter a city and destroy every man and woman, young and old, plus all the cattle and donkeys.

What I do remember from the morning is, somewhere in the middle of the sermon, the preacher decided to read this verse on the slaughter of people and livestock. Out loud.

I was sitting in a back pew with a non-Christian friend. I had just begun attending church again after several years' absence. I called myself a Christian, but my life argued otherwise.

When the preacher moved to read this text, it was like watching a car crash. Have you ever seen one? For half a second, the world tunnel-visions toward the catastrophe about to happen. The action moves slowly from one frame to the next. Things grow eerily silent. Then BAM!

Except the bam was a human voice, and it lasted through the duration of the verse. The preacher read it, and looked up at us.

He paused.

It was now completely silent.

I felt a surreal mixture of embarrassment and fascination. Embarrassed by what my friend might be thinking. Fascinated by what might come next. The biblical text was reality-exploding. God just told His people to destroy . . . an entire city. Yes, this was a unique moment in redemptive history, not directly applicable to the church, but . . . but . . . what do you do with a God who would *ever* make such a command?

For as difficult as these biblical words were to hear, it was the preacher's next words that really made the biblical text press down on me: "If you are a Christian, you should know why a verse like this is in the Bible."

Excuse me? I should know why this is in the Bible? What do you mean I should know? You're the preacher. You should know!

But that's not the game he was playing. He put the text on me, and on everyone else listening. He didn't seem embarrassed by what God had just said. He didn't make excuses for it, like one does with an aging and senile parent who just said something inappropriate. No, he just read the verse and told us that we needed to deal with it. The text was finally our responsibility.

Somehow I relaxed. It made sense. No, I couldn't explain why such a verse was in the Bible, but, to be sure, it was saying something exceptionally significant about both God and humanity. And a true Christian needs to figure out what to do with it. The verse is there. You can say the Bible has mistakes, or you can figure out how to place this particular beam into the structure of your faith.

I don't remember what the preacher said after that. But my world had already been changed. Reality had been reordered. I was seeing with a slightly different set of eyes, kind of like the new perspectives one acquires with age, but in an instant.

That's what biblical preaching will do. The Word confronts your present reality, and then the Spirit gives you a new one.

Applying or Confronting?

Just about any book you find on preaching or studying God's Word will talk about the importance of "application." Application, Daniel Overdorf helpfully puts it, "explains or demonstrates how biblical teaching should impact the lives of contemporary listeners." It "leads the listeners to imagine how the truth of the text makes a difference to where they live."[1]

> *Throughout Scripture, God commands us to obey, listen, and repent. He confronts our self-rule.*

Now that we have considered the *announcement* of preaching in the last chapter, it seems like *application* is what we'd want to consider in this one. People don't need just an explanation of a biblical text, they need some idea of what it means in their particular situations.

In a sense, that's what we're going to consider in this chapter, but I want to approach the matter from a slightly different angle, namely, through the lens of *confrontation*. In the illustration above, you could say the preacher "applied" the text in Joshua, or you could say he confronted us with it. Either is fine, but in my mind the latter more broadly represents what's happening. Throughout Scripture, God commands us to obey, listen, and repent. He confronts our self-rule. A preacher then does the same. In exposing Scripture, he exposes its confrontation.

The language of application works when we regard words as little vessels of information that sail from one brain to another through the act of speaking. Give me data that I don't have, and I will apply it. Notice the emphasis is on the preacher and the listener's activity. It's on the human half of the equation. The preacher applies the text, and the listener applies it to his life. It also treats the human problem as one of ignorance.

But there's more happening than just this. God has invested Himself in His Word. And God acts through His Word. In the Bible, God encounters us, and He changes us. Ignorance is indeed one of our problems, but even worse is the stiff neck and puffed-out chest of our self-rule. God gives us new information in the Scriptures, but He also confronts us with His crown. He confronts our idols and false gods. He confronts our pride and fear. He confronts our pain and weakness. He confronts our autonomy and impulse to self-help. He confronts the lies and false realities that we dearly love. Most fundamentally, He confronts our self-rule.

And then—amazing grace!—He breaks that self-rule. I was blind, but now I see.

God does all this when we pick up His Word to read it by ourselves. He also does this through the Sunday preacher.

No other medium of communication works quite like this. Present me with the picture of a pretty face, or the sound of a sweet melody, and my mind and heart can become engaged, yes, but apart from words, there is no challenge to my self-sovereignty. Only words—and especially words from a king—can call me to surrender my will.

That's why our churches must be utterly centered upon God's words. If our basic problem is self-rule, then we must be confronted again and again at the point of our wrong allegiance, and called to a better allegiance. Sometimes God's words confront us with a needed rebuke; sometimes they confront us with assurance or comfort. Yet in every case, the message is the same: "You won't find what you're looking for, whether correction or comfort, in yourself, your rule, or your resources."

Now, my emphasis on confrontation doesn't mean that a teacher of God's Word must not situate himself *with* or *among* God's people. No, he, too, must sit *under* God's Word *with* God's people, and he should administer the confrontation of God's Word to God's people with unaffected empathy: "God says this to *us*." Nor does my emphasis on confrontation mean to diminish the significance of the Word making His dwelling *among* us.

But I do very much mean to say that God the Son made His dwelling among us *not* to leave us as we are, but to call us to repent and follow in the way of the Father through the instruction of the Son and the power of the Spirit.

So it comes to this: After hearing words that announce what God has done, we need to hear words of confrontation, which is the preacher's task.

Scripture's Confrontation: An Illustration

Framing this chapter in terms of *confrontation*, I understand, is deeply out of sync with our culture. Confronting other people is not what we do today. But the fact is, the Bible is fundamentally confrontational. I'm not just referring to its commands and exhortations—its *thou-shalt-nots*. I'm referring to every single verse. The Bible as a whole—get this!—says that you're not who you think you are. And God is not who you think He is. And then it calls us to exchange the story we've been telling ourselves with God's version of our story. It redefines reality, or gives us new eyes. As Moses put it, the words of the Bible "are not just idle words for you—they are your *life*" (Deut. 32:47 NIV, italics added).

Before we ever read the Bible, we all have stories that we use to define ourselves and the world around us. Imagine several people who might be sitting next to you on a Sunday morning, and imagine what their stories might sound like:

"I'm Frank. I'm an urban professional. I enjoy my job and make a lot of money. My parents were nice, and I'm nice. I'm basically a good person. People like me because I'm funny. That makes me feel good. My life's going pretty well so I don't see the point of religion. I believe you can choose your own morality, just so long as you don't step on someone else's toes. So I live my life the way I want."

"I'm Kaitlyn. My dad was mean and abusive. My mom became an alcoholic, and became mean herself. I hate both of them. I'm cynical and needy because of them, and I feel helpless to change. Sometimes my therapist makes me feel better but then it wears off. I don't believe in organized religion or God, at least as a person. But I do believe life is spiritual and God is in everyone and everything."

"I'm Dwayne. I've grown up in the church. I've always been a Christian. I'm a really good person. I'm not bad or rebellious like Frank or Kaitlyn."

These are the stories that Frank, Kaitlyn, and Dwayne tell themselves. This is how they interpret reality—themselves, God, life's purpose, and morality.

But open the Bible and God's words of announcement and confrontation begin in the very first verse: "In the beginning, God created the heavens and the earth." The first thing to notice about the verse is its subject: God. The creation account is primarily about God. Indeed, if we keep reading, we'll discover that the story of the whole Bible is about God. God is the main character. God is the protagonist. God is the "good guy" who will win in the end.

This first verse also tells us that God is all-powerful. Nothing existed. Then it did. It tells us God is eternal. He existed "before" the beginning. And it tells us that God is utterly self-sufficient. He created everything from the workshop of His own mind.

If all these things are true, God doesn't owe us. He cannot be manipulated by our demands, our claims, or our boasts. He is not beholden to us, and we have no rights independent of Him.

All of this is *announced*, you might say, in the first verse of the Bible, particularly if we're reading the verse together with the Bible's own commentary on this verse (e.g. Ps. 50:10–12; Acts 17:24–25).

How do these announcements then *confront* Frank, Kaitlyn, and Dwayne? Consider their stories once more. All three are the main characters—the good guys—in their own story. They think the universe is about them, and that morality is defined by them. For Frank, everything that affords pleasure is good. For Kaitlyn, everything that affords healing is good. For Dwayne, everything that allows him to continue vindicating his own name is good. And it's not hard to imagine how their entire lives will warp around these value systems.

But Genesis 1:1 shines the light on their make-believe worlds. It tells them that the universe doesn't exist to serve them, and that right and wrong are not defined by them. It says that they live in God's universe, and they are utterly beholden to Him and the glory of His name. Pleasure, healing, and justification occur on His terms and will yield all glory to Him (because they are granted by faith). All three characters, in conclusion, have been living and believing in a way that's out of sync with reality. Genesis 1:1 is reality.

So it is with all of Scripture. It gives us reality.

The Preacher's Confrontation

The preacher's task, then, is to articulate this confrontation. He holds up reality as the Bible presents it, and asks how it compares to what his hearers have been calling reality. He asks the Franks, Kaitlyns, and Dwaynes if all the promises that sin has been making to them have turned out to be true. He shows them that the Bible is, in fact, a better interpreter of their experience. And then he points them to the warnings and promises that it personally makes to them.

Doing this well, of course, means the preacher must understand what his hearers believe—the warp and woof of their false worlds. His goal is to confront those beliefs precisely. Here are four categories that influence every person and which the preacher must confront:

First, worldviews. Often a person's response to Scripture is dictated by worldview presuppositions that he or she is not even aware of. Philippians tells us to look to the interests of others (2:3–5), but to what extent does our materialism limit how sacrificially we're willing to do this? Hebrews 13:17 tells us to submit to our leaders, but does our individualism and radical egalitarianism hinder our ability to heed such a command? Jesus tells us to take up our crosses (Luke 9:23–25), but are we too loaded down with entitlements to hear Him? A preacher does not need to use words like "consumerism," "relativism," "naturalism," and "emotivism." But he should know how to expose and disarm them.

Second, spiritual state. I assume that every listener, at some level, struggles with *idolatry, self-justification,* and *the love of the world.* A preacher should always do battle with these enemies. At the same time, preachers must preach to people in different spiritual states. Paul identifies the *idle,* the *timid,* and the *weak,* each of whom require slightly different challenges (1 Thess. 5:12–14).

When I'm planning my sermons or Bible study lessons, I also try to think through three sets of pairs. I want to address both *Christians and non-Christians.* I want to address both the *complacent and needy.* And I want to address both the *legalistic and hedonistic.* Each of these categories requires a different kind of challenge. The complacent need to hear God's warnings, while the needy need to hear His promises. The legalistic need to hear about grace, while the licentious may need to be challenged by imperatives. The difficulty, of course, is to challenge one side of the pair while not causing the other side to stumble.

I might have erred too far in one direction in a recent devotion that I gave. I offered a challenge which was intended (in my mind) for the complacent crowd. But after the sermon one helpful brother observed that my challenge might have caused undue grief among those who are especially guilt-prone. If I ever give that particular devotion again, I may offer the same challenge, but I'll qualify it more carefully.

Third, social state. In preparing a sermon, a preacher should consider how to aim the burden of the text at different kinds of people: What does the text mean for men or for women? For children and adults? For people moving toward retirement? For people who make a lot of money? For people who struggle to pay the bills? For employers and employees? For singles, marrieds, and widowed? For members of a minority ethnicity and the majority ethnicity? For foreigners? For parents? People encounter the Word differently depending on their station or season of life. A good teacher wants to help them wherever they are.

Fourth, corporate meaning. In preaching or teaching, I find that it's comparatively easy to address people as *individuals.* You ask them what they're hoping in. You help them to see the connection between their hopes and how they treat their spouses. And so forth. What's harder, at least in our individualistic day, is to confront the congregation *corporately*—to present the church with a picture of the corporate reality to which God calls His people. But that's how Jesus confronts His disciples: "By this all people will know that you are my disciples, *if you have love for one another*" (John 13:35, italics added).

The apostle Paul seems to say that one of the main purposes of preaching is to build up the body in its togetherness. Pastors and teachers, he says, are "to equip the saints for the work of ministry, for building up the body of Christ, until we all attain to the unity of the faith and of the knowledge of the Son of God, to mature manhood" (Eph. 4:12–13). One of the main goals of preaching is to equip the saints in such a way that they are built up in their life *together.*

The same message shows up in Paul's discussion of spiritual gifts in 1 Corinthians 12 to 14 as he emphasizes those gifts which build up the body.

This corporate dimension is relevant not just for preaching John 13 or Ephesians 4, but for every text of Scripture. When preparing a sermon or lesson, teachers of God's Word should always ask themselves, "How does this text call us to greater unity as a church, and the employment of our gifts in service to one another?"

Him, Not Us

Preaching involves "application," no doubt. You *apply* an ancient text to different kinds of contemporary people. You help them to understand its relevance in their lives. But here's what must be utterly plain to preachers and churches: The real action occurs whenever the biblical text *confronts* a listener accompanied by Holy Spirit power. You don't tell your congregation to go home, apply such and such a text to their lives, and wait for remarkable results to occur, like it's some sort of antiaging lotion. Most often, I suspect, the Word does its true work right there in the moment of preaching.

Then and there, the Word awakens the dead heart. It gives hearing to the deaf ears. It gives sight to the blind. Or it calluses and hardens (Isa. 6:9–10). And once these things are accomplished, they're accomplished. You don't need to tell the newly seeing to see, or the newly hearing to hear. The change has happened. God has done it.

So expose the Word. Announce it. Confront people with it.

I believe this is what Paul was getting at when he said, "My speech and my message were not in plausible words of wisdom, but in demonstration of the Spirit and of power" (1 Cor. 2:4). And it's why he could say, "We have received not the spirit of this world, but the Spirit who is from God, that we might understand the things freely given us by God. And we impart this in words not taught by human wisdom but taught by the Spirit" (2:12–13). The Spirit *teaches.* And once He does, the task is done. God can use the charisma, rhetorical skill, or fine arguments of preachers, but these things don't break and re-create hearts. God's Word and Spirit do.

So expose the Word. Announce it. Confront people with

it. And then let the Spirit soften or harden their hearts as He pleases. As Paul said, "I planted, Apollos watered, but God gave the growth" (1 Cor. 3:6).

That was me, sitting in a back pew with a non-Christian friend, when I heard the text in Joshua, coupled with the preacher's challenge. At that moment, reality shifted before my eyes. My universe was a little less me-centered and a little more God-centered by the time the sermon was over.

Sometimes, of course, the Spirit will work after the fact. Two months might pass after a sermon, and then some phrase will jump into your mind and pierce the conscience afresh. Either way, Luther's oft-quoted account of the Protestant Reformation is surely instructive: "I simply taught, preached, wrote God's Word: otherwise I did nothing. And then, while I slept or drank Wittenberg beer with my Philip of Amsdorf, the Word so greatly weakened the papacy that never a prince or emperor did such damage to it. I did nothing: the Word did it all."[2]

Notes

1. Daniel Overdorf, *Applying the Sermon: How to Balance Biblical Integrity and Cultural Relevance* (Grand Rapids: Kregel, 2009), 21.

2. Martin Luther, as quoted in Reformation Theology. Posted 20 March 2009: www.reformation theology.com/2009/03/the_word_did_it_all_martin_lut.php.

Recommended Reading

Johnson, Darrell W. *The Glory of Preaching: Participating in God's Transformation of the World.* Downers Grove, Ill.: InterVarsity, 2009.

Mohler, R. Albert. *He Is Not Silent: Preaching in a Postmodern World.* Chicago: Moody, 2008.

Overdorff, Daniel. *Applying the Sermon.* Grand Rapids: Kregel, 2009.

PART 3
the
reverberation

8 } the reverberation sings

At my church's Sunday gathering, the preacher and everyone leading the service sit on the stage facing the congregation. They take their turns at the pulpit for announcements, song introductions, and so on. Otherwise, they're looking at you, and you're looking at them.

I'm not sure why our church does it this way, other than that's how we've always done it.

What's slightly awkward is that they continually glance around at the congregation. It looks like they're people-watching, like you might do at a shopping mall. Who's walking in? Who's sitting next to whom? What's he wearing?

In the past, I've been tempted to wonder if they're

really worshiping, or just looking around. Doesn't someone who is *really* worshiping close his eyes, put up his hands, and wear an expression of rapture? He's lost to the world, and the world's lost to him, because it's just him and Jesus now. Never mind the several hundred other people in the room. Just keep the music looping.

At least that's what I wondered until it was me sitting on stage, looking out at the congregation.

Now, I confess I do a little people watching—who's walking in and who sits next to whom. But that's only during the announcements. When the singing begins, I'm doing something else entirely: I'm beholding God's people praise God. And it's unbelievable!

Some eyes are closed and some are open. Some hands are raised and some are not. But the posture of their bodies is not the point.

The point is, as one of their shepherds, I know some of what's happening in their lives. I know a few of their individual struggles and joys, and now I have a front row seat to watch them pour out their born-again hearts to their Comforter and Rock in the midst of those struggles and joys.

What I Behold

We're singing the sixteenth-century words of "A Mighty Fortress," and I notice a woman who was recently assaulted now sing with all her might of a "bulwark never failing."

We're singing the eighteenth-century words of "Come, Thou Fount of Every Blessings" and I'm heartened by the older saint who has persevered in the faith for decades, still singing, "prone to wander, Lord, I feel it, prone to leave the God I love; here's my heart, O, take and seal it; seal it for thy courts above."

We're singing the nineteenth-century words of "It Is Well with My Soul," and I look out and see the middle-aged brother struggling with discouragement over his fight against sinful anger now raising his voice to shout, "My sin—oh, the bliss of this glorious thought: my sin, not in part, but the whole is nailed to the cross and I bear it no more, Praise the Lord, praise the Lord, O my soul!"

Singing in the church is about listening as much as it's about singing.

We're singing the twenty-first century words of "In Christ Alone," and I see the talented young mother who is tempted to regret what she's given up to have children now exult in her new ambition: "In Christ alone my hope is found, he is my light, my strength, my song."

As I sit, look out, and behold, my own praises to God are strengthened by the stories and songs of others. My faith is invigorated and enlarged by His work in *them*.

The Echoing Word

Christians in our churches sing because their new hearts can't help but echo the Word that has given them life. Whether those songs were written in the sixteenth century or today, they should echo Scripture. If there is any place where God's Word should literally reverberate, it should reverberate in the church's songs. Remember, Scripture alone gives life. Therefore, a church's songs should contain nothing more than the words, paraphrases, or ideas of Scripture.

And Christians sing *together* because it helps us to see that our hearts' praises, confessions, and resolutions are shared. We're not alone. Singing in the church, I believe, is about listening as much as it's about singing. So Paul commands us to "*Speak to one another* with psalms, hymns and spiritual songs. Sing and make music in your heart to the Lord" (Eph. 5:19

NIV). If I'm to speak to others in song, I'm to listen to others as well. In fact, I *do* sometimes stop singing just to listen and thank God for the voices around me!

You might think of the dim and temporary unity all the home team fans experience as they root for their team at a football game. Together they rise to their feet and cheer.

How much more should a church of Jesus Christ both enjoy and display its unity when it sings! These brothers and sisters share our new identities, our Lord and Savior, our comfort and support, our hope and our joy. You're with them, they're with you, and we're with Him.

Why We Sing

Believers sing in churches because Christ has commanded us to sing together (Col. 3:16; Eph. 5:19). And we're commanded to sing, I heard minister of music Bob Kauflin observe, because God means for creatures created in His image to do as He does (e.g., Zeph. 3:17; Heb. 2:12). Let me offer three reasons why God would command His people to speak to one another not just in prose, but in poetry and melody.

We Sing to Own and Affirm the Word

Singing is how the congregation owns and affirms the Word for itself. In the Bible, singing is one God-ordained way for the members of a congregation to respond to God's revelation. It's how they raise their hand and say, "Yes, I believe and affirm these truths with my whole person." For instance, the psalmist tells God's people to proclaim God's Word to others: "Sing to the Lord, bless his name; tell of his salvation from day to day" (Ps. 96:2). Singing of His salvation means we've owned it as our message.

We Sing to Engage Our Emotions with God's Word

Singing is how the congregation particularly engages its emotions and affections with God's Word. When we sing, it's hard to remain emotionally disengaged. Just as the sense of smell can evoke strong associations and memories, so the sound of music both evokes and provokes the heart's joys, griefs, longings, hopes, and sorrows. Jonathan Edwards proposed that God gave us music "wholly to excite and express religious affections." The psalmist seems to embody this idea when he writes, "My heart overflows with a pleasing theme" (Ps. 45:1).

Singing, I'd say, is the medium by which God's people grab hold of His Word and align their emotions and affections to God's.

It's not surprising, therefore, that Paul would command churches to sing the psalms, and that the Psalter would be referred to as the church's hymnbook. John Calvin called the Psalms "An Anatomy of All the Parts of the Soul" since it offers readers words which they can place into their own mouths for properly expressing the whole range of human emotions. In the preface to his commentary on the Psalms, Calvin writes, "For there is not an emotion of which any one can be conscious that is not here represented as in a mirror. Or rather, the Holy Spirit has here drawn to the life all the griefs, sorrows, fears, doubts, hopes, cares, perplexities, in short, all the distracting emotions with which the minds of men are wont to be agitated."[1] How can Christians express grief in godly fashion? Or sorrow, fear, and doubt? By echoing the Psalms, like Jesus did again and again.

Yet even if churches don't take their lyrics directly from the Psalter, they should consider the Psalms' balance of confession, lamentation, exaltation, and thanksgiving, and seek to mimic something similar in their own hymnody. Do we know how to lament in our churches through music? Or confess?

In seminary classrooms, budding preachers are sometimes warned, "A congregation will only be as careful with the Word as you are in the pulpit." The same is true, I'm convinced, of our singing in church, and our ability to emotionally encounter God throughout the week. A congregation that learns to sing in church with robust confession and contrite praise better knows how to sing to God with their hearts at home, whether they do it to melody or not.

We Sing to Demonstrate and Build Unity

Singing is one way of demonstrating and building corporate unity. Once again, it's not difficult to imagine how Israel used the Psalms to demonstrate and build the unity of their hearts with one another. Some psalms make this explicit:

> **Call:**
> *Oh give thanks to the Lord, for he is good;*
> *for his steadfast love endures forever!*
> **Response 1:**
> Let Israel say, "*His steadfast love endures forever.*"
> **Response 2:**
> Let the house of Aaron say, "*His steadfast love endures forever.*"
> **Response 3:**
> Let those who fear the Lord say, "*His steadfast love endures forever.*" (Psalm 118:1–4; see also 124:1; 129:1; 136)

The psalmist makes a declaration, and then he asks three groups of people to echo him: the nation, the priests, and then all who fear God (including any foreigners and Gentiles in their midst). The words "his steadfast love endures forever" is the source of unity, but the poetry and—perhaps—music encourages the people's hearts to embrace, own, and rejoice in this glorious truth.

The context of Paul's command to sing is worth noticing as well: "And let the peace of Christ rule in your hearts, to which indeed you were called in one body. And be thankful. Let the word of Christ dwell in you richly . . . singing psalms and hymns and spiritual songs, with thankfulness in your hearts to God" (Col. 3:15–16). Notice the train of thought: We're to let peace rule, since we're called to one body. We're to be thankful. And we can do all this by singing Christ's Word together. Again, the Word is the source of unity; but the music gives expression to that unity.

No doubt, this point can be combined with the last one. Singing God's Word is how a congregation tunes its heart together across the whole range of biblically driven affections.

What should be clear in all three reasons for why we sing is that singing in church should be about the church singing—congregational singing. Perhaps choirs and soloists can be carefully used to call the church to respond, as in the psalm above or as an exercise in "speaking to one another in song." And musical performances *outside* the gathered church are wonderful. But God has given music to the *gathered* church so that the people together can own, affirm, rejoice in, and unite around God's Word. Far better than the sweet harmonies of a few trained singers is the rough and hale sound of pardoned criminals, delighting with one voice in their Savior.

The most beautiful instrument in any Christian service is the sound of the congregation singing.

Reprogramming Our Hearts

More reasons could be listed for why Christians sing, and why Christians should together sing Scripture's words, ideas, and paraphrases. Kauflin writes that, in addition to engaging the emotions and building unity, singing provides an easier way to commit the truths of Scripture to memory, and that it anticipates the songs to come (Rev. 5:9–10).[2] Primarily, singing is a God-ordained means for echoing God's Word back and forth to one another in a way that engages the whole person—heart, mind, affections, and will. We should not use music to create something that the Word has not created, say, by riling up the emotions with triumphalistic music. (Performance music in churches often seems to do this.) Rather, churches should use music to train believers in the experience of sanctified, Word-driven emotions and affections.

It's a lesson, in other words, to take home. The melodious reverberations of God's Word in song should echo out the church doors and into our friendships and homes. We should sing throughout the week.

But more than that, the reverberations of singing God's Word, I dare say, should begin to reprogram the very way in which a Christian experiences emotion and affection. We can let our emotions be trained by sports enthusiasm, by television commercials, by movies, by the songs on the radio, by whatever our culture defines as masculine or feminine. Or we can let our emotional lives be formed by the church's singing of God's Word, by the Psalms, by centuries of wonderful hymnody, and by the choruses of the saints today.

Do we know what it is to weep with David that God's laws are not kept (Ps. 119:136)? Do we know how to let cheerfulness turn into a song of praise, as James commends (James 5:13)? Does the thought of our sin being nailed to the cross provoke feelings of "bliss" in us, as it did for Horatio Spafford, author of "It Is Well with My Soul"?

Singing with Brad

My friend Brad helped me to do a little reprogramming of my own heart. Brad was a fellow member of a former church of mine, and we met weekly for a season. I remember one evening driving up to his house to pick him up for dinner, and he was waiting for me on the curb. I reached over, opened the car door from the inside, and heard him immediately say, "Hey, Jonathan, have you ever seen a CD player this small?" He had brought his own battery-powered player and was intending to play it. But it wasn't that small.

Brad is autistic and blind. Like most people with autism, he's socially awkward, and makes strange bodily movements. For instance, he will squeeze his eyes shut, flap his hands in front of his face so that his finger tips touch, and then repeatedly wipe his face with both hands.

I turned my car radio off. Brad's finger hit the play button. We had not made much conversation at that point. We had not said hello. Still, it was time to sing. Not two more seconds passed and the Atlanta Symphony Chorus began filling the small cabin of my car with Handel's "Hallelujah Chorus," accompanied by Brad's own sonorous vibrato. Brad may be blind and autistic, but he's also a member of a professional chorus and has a beautiful voice.

"Hallelujah . . . Hallelujah . . . For the Lord God omnipotent . . ."

I began singing with him. My meager baritone was no match for his hardy tenor.

"The kingdom of this world is become the kingdom of our Lord and of his Christ; and he shall reign for ever and ever." The cabin reverberated loudly with these words from the book of Revelation.

I began thinking about this King of kings who had established His kingdom in Brad's heart.

The song finished. Brad then asked me, "Do you know this one?" He punched the track button, and then he sang the following lines from Isaiah that Handel placed in part two of his *Messiah*: "He was wounded for our transgressions, he was bruised for our iniquities; the chastisement of our peace was upon him; and with his stripes we are healed."

But Brad didn't let the song finish. He stopped the CD in order to discuss the lyrics with me. "Yep, with His stripes we are healed. Do you know that, Jonathan? With His stripes we are healed. He was bruised for our iniquities. And with His stripes we are healed. He took the suffering we deserved. He paid for our sins. With His stripes we are healed."

He talked this way for several minutes. Actually, he talked this way most of the evening. There was no pretense in his words. There was no fear in what I might think of him. He simply spoke gospel. Gospel words from gospel lips overflowing from a gospel heart. I wondered at several points if I was with a prophet.

The clear ring of Brad's heart was a sermon to me.

Make no mistake, Brad is lonely. He longs for more friends. He longs for a wife. He longs to see. He longs to be released from the ravages of a crumpled nervous system.

Yet, somehow, more than any of these things, he longs for the day when he will be released from sin and the ravages of sin. That evening, in fact, it occurred to me that Brad's heart rang like a gospel bell, ringing this one sustained note. You know what a bell sounds like. There is no complexity, no dissonance, no conflict in its ring. A bell's sound is not boastful.

It does not presume to be an orchestra. A bell is single-minded and wills only one thing: to sing its one note clearly.

"By His stripes we are healed," Brad kept saying.

He told me that his mom tries to get him to stop talking about the gospel so much. I wasn't surprised. This evening wasn't unique. Brad often talks this way. He cannot help it.

I considered my own mind and heart: analytical, complex, fickle, double-minded, occasionally afraid. I wish the people closest to me got sick of hearing me talk about the gospel so much.

The apostle Paul's words also rang in my ears that night: God chose the foolish things of the world to shame the wise, and the things that are not to nullify the things that are (1 Cor. 1:27).

Amidst the jumble of words and sentences, the clear ring of Brad's heart was a sermon to me. Brad exhorted me. He reminded me of my sins. He pointed me to the one thing I must will and re-will and re-will—to be possessed by Him who is most pure and perfect, and by whose stripes I have been healed.

Brad sang to me, and helped me to sing. And we rejoiced together over the King of kings and Lord of lords who is establishing His kingdom both among the foolish and blind, like me, and the wise and clear-sighted, like Brad.

Notes

1. John Calvin, *Commentary on the Book of Psalms*, trans. James Anderson, vol. 4 (Grand Rapids: Baker, 1981), xxxvii.

2. Bob Kauflin, "Words of Wonder: What Happens When We Sing," in *The Power of Words and the Wonder of God*, ed. John Piper and Justin Taylor, (Wheaton, Ill.: Crossway, 2009), 124–27, 134–35. Kauflin is director of worship for Sovereign Grace Ministries.

Recommended Reading

Ashton, Mark, D. A. Carson, R. Kent Hughes and Timothy J. Keller. *Worship by the Book.* Grand Rapids:Zondervan, 2002. Chapter 1.

Dever, Mark and Michael Lawrence. *Perspectives on Christian Worship.* J. Matthew Pinson, ed. Nashville: B&H, 2009. Chapter 7 ("Blended Worship").

Duncan, J. Ligon and Derek W. H. Thomas, eds. *Give Praise to God: A Vision for Reforming Worship.* Phillipsburg, N.J.: P&R, 2003.

Kauflin, Bob. *Worship Matters: Leading Others to Encounter the Greatness of God.* Wheaton, Ill.: Crossway, 2008.

9 } the reverberation prays

A church's prayer list will tell you a lot about that church and its members. Many church prayer lists that I've seen look like this:

> *Don't forget to pray for*
> Suzy's upcoming shoulder surgery.
> The Mason twins' laryngitis.
> The senior ladies' Sunday school bake sale.
> The Thomases' sale of their home.
> The youth group's carwash.
> The Robinsons, our missionaries in Ecuador.
> Summer jobs for our high school students.
> Bill's pneumonia.
> Bill's aunt's double-pneumonia.
> Unspoken requests.

When I first arrived in Kentucky for seminary, I joined a small Baptist church that had a prayer list much like this one. The vast majority of items were health requests (I've under-represented the percentage here). Few of the items were relevant to the church as a whole, except for one or two "ministry" requests, like a missionary known only to the one member of the missions committee. And the person who read the list in our church's Wednesday night prayer services never failed to have us raise our hands for "unspoken requests."

This last category amazed me. If you're not going to share the request, so that the church can own it with you, what good is acknowledging an "unspoken request"?

In fact, I think this category reveals something about how many churches and Christians view prayer. Prayer is a mechanism for inducing the Almighty to do what you want, and it's essentially a private exercise.

Our prayers reveal what our hearts want.

J. I. Packer is surely right when he says that "prayer is the measure of a man, spiritually, in a way that nothing else is."[1] Our prayers reveal what our hearts want. They reveal how we regard God, His glory, and His power. And they reveal the quality and measure of faith—do we pray often and carefully, or not much at all? The same must be true of a church's prayers. They reveal what a church truly values, and where it places its hope.

In chapter 8, we considered how God's Word should reverberate in a church's singing. We said that singing is the medium by which God's people grab hold of His Word and align their affections and emotions to His. In the same way, God's Word should reverberate through the church's prayers. Praying is how God's people should grab hold of His Word and align their will and their hopes with His.

Pagans pray, no doubt. They ask God for things. But a key difference between a Christian and a non-Christian's praying is that Christian praying will increasingly conform to the intentions of God's Word. So we will adore, confess, give thanks, and ask for those things which His Word tells us to. We are the people who delight ourselves in the Lord, and so He places new desires in our hearts, desires that He then fulfills when we ask for them through prayer (Ps. 37:4).

Here are three lessons that Jesus teaches about prayer.

Christians Should Pray for the Sake of God's Name

First and foremost, Christians should pray for the sake of God's name. Our Holy Spirit-indwelled hearts will desire that God's glory be displayed on the earth. So we will pray together with our Lord Jesus, "Our Father in heaven, hallowed be your name" (Matt. 6:9).

Praying for God's glory is not "Advanced Christianity." It's not "Praying for Jonathan Edwards Enthusiasts." It's Praying 101. It's bound up in the very kernel of our faith and salvation. We are justified by faith, said the apostle Paul, in order to exclude all boasting (Rom. 3:27). To seek justification through faith, in other words, is to surrender our quest for the glory of our own names. We're no longer saying, "Look at me and my merit!" We're now saying, "I surrender my quest for glory and self-justification. Have mercy and save me *for the sake of your great name*" (see Ps. 79:9; Isa. 45:25; Ezek. 36:22). Whether we could articulate it or not, that's the prayer of every child of God at conversion.

When we lift up our *praises* and *thanksgivings*, we are saying "Hallowed be your name" (Matt. 6:9).

When we lift up our *confessions* of sin, we are saying the same thing, since we know that we have fallen short of His glory (see Rom. 3:23).

Even when we lift up our *requests*, we are praying that God's name would be hallowed. As Daniel prayed, "O Lord, pay attention and act. Delay not, for your own sake, O my God, because your city and your people are called by your name" (Dan. 9:19; see also Ex. 32:11–13). Notice in Daniel's prayer the source of our salvation—the fact that our covenanting God ties His name to ours. He stakes His reputation on our good. And so His covenant people can pray "Hallowed be your name" knowing that it will be the source of their own salvation and glory.

The words "Hallowed be your name" precede everything else in the Lord's Prayer because, in lifting our requests to God, we make it possible for God to glorify Himself by answering our prayers in mercy and power.

Now admittedly, God's glory is not what I desire every time I open my mouth to pray. And to whatever extent I don't desire His glory, I am praying like a non-Christian. I am asking wrongly for the sake of my passions (James 4:3). The Holy Spirit-given prayer of faith, on the other hand, is always a prayer for God's glory, because that's what the Holy Spirit desires.

As individuals and as churches, therefore, we should do all we can to align our prayers to Scripture's grand ambition— the glory of God.

Christians Should Pray for God's Rule and Will on Earth

Christians should also pray that God's rule and will would be done on the earth. Again, we pray together with our Lord Jesus, "Your kingdom come, your will be done, on earth as it is in heaven" (Matt. 6:10).

Christians often wonder about how to discern God's will, but the Lord's Prayer tells us what it is: God's will is that His kingdom rule would be displayed unto the ends of the earth; He wants humanity to worship and obey Him even as the angels of heaven do.

Here, indeed, is another point of difference between a Christian prayer and a non-Christian prayer. Christian prayers are informed by this desire to see God's kingdom rule expanded and displayed—the desire to see God's will done on earth. That's certainly how our Lord prayed in His own ministry: "Not my will, but yours, be done" (Luke 22:42).

Christian prayer seeks first the kingdom of God and His righteousness. More concretely, it's interested in evangelism and conversion. It's interested in the holiness and love of God's people, and their willingness to make decisions that look strange to the world. It's interested in the health of the local church, and its commitment to expositional preaching. It's interested in the success of other nearby churches, and not just one's own, because we're all playing for the same team. It's interested in Christians going into their workplaces and working as unto Christ, and in husbands and wives living as distinctively *Christian* husbands and wives. It's interested in the preaching of the gospel in foreign nations, and the ability to gather freely for worship, and in the plight of persecuted brothers and sisters around the world.

It wouldn't be quite right to say that kingdom-oriented prayers are simply interested in the next life, and not this one. After all, the prayer is for the kingdom to *come*, and for God's will to be done *on earth*, both of which seem to imply *now*. Which means born-again Christian hearts should increasingly desire to make disciples of Christ and to see Christ's disciples living according to "the obedience of faith" (Rom. 1:5). The kingdom comes to earth whenever and wherever Christians are living in the obedience of faith by the power of the Spirit for the sake of Jesus' name.

As individuals and as churches, therefore, we should do all we can to align our prayers to God's will and kingdom purposes. How then do we as individuals and churches ensure that we're praying according to God's will, and for kingdom priorities?

Christians Should Pray According to Scriptural Priorities

The answer is easy: pray Scripture, or according to Scriptural priorities and patterns. Let the words and agenda of the Bible reverberate into your individual and corporate prayer life.

It's not surprising, then, that Paul prays for one church, "We constantly pray for you . . . that by his power he may fulfill every good purpose of yours and every act prompted by your faith" (2 Thess. 1:11 NIV). It's like Paul is saying to them, "If you want what God wants, then I want it too!"

The latter half of the Lord's Prayer offers three sets of priorities: "Give us this day our daily bread, and forgive us our debts, as we also have forgiven our debtors. And lead us not into temptation, but deliver us from evil" (Matt. 6:11–13). First, we should ask God to provide our daily needs. It reminds us that we're utterly dependent upon Him in all things. But notice, we're not just interested in seeing our own children fed. We should pray that children of others are fed—give us *our* bread. Second, we should ask to be forgiven of sin, and to have the ability to forgive others. And third, we should ask for holiness and the ability to flee sin.

Notice that each of these latter requests take on a corporate dimension. Jesus says "*our* debts" and "deliver *us*." Christian maturity means incorporating more and more of Christ's attitude into our desires, hopes, laments, griefs, rejoicing, and even our identity. Just as a man's identity changes from "I" to "We" when he enters the one-flesh union of marriage or becomes a father, so a non-Christian's identity changes from "I" to "We" when he becomes a Christian. He's now part of a family. This means that the prayers of a born-again heart will increasingly be burdened for others, and not just oneself. It also means we should practice praying *with* our congregations, so that we are indeed praying to *our* Father.

The Psalms are good to pray, of course. But so is all of Scripture. Paul's prayers in particular are worth imitating.

- He prays that the Ephesians would be given the spiritual sight to see the glorious inheritance awaiting God's saints (1:16–19).
- He prays that the Philippians' love would become more discerning and knowledgeable so that they might pursue only good things and live holy lives (1:9–11).
- He prays that the Colossians would be filled with the knowledge of God's will so that they might live pleasing lives of good works and growth in the knowledge of God (1:9–10).
- Paul also calls on others to pray for his own evangelism (Col. 4:3–4; 2 Thess. 3:1–2).

Do our churches pray this way? Do we individually? More examples could be given, and the reader would do well to pick up D. A. Carson's *A Call to Spiritual Reformation: Priorities from Paul and His Prayers*, which meditates profoundly on how Paul's desires should shape our own.

The point here is that there's a vast difference between Jesus' or Paul's bullet-pointed prayer list and the list of most churches, such as the one at the beginning of this chapter. No doubt it's good to pray for health concerns, and jobs, and home sales. But the heart which is growing with the prayer "Your will be done on earth as it is in heaven" is praying for much, much more.

We should align our prayers to the priorities and patterns of the Bible.

Praying Scripture means that church leaders might want to consider preparing their prayers in advance rather than place such a high premium on that quintessential virtue of Romanticism (and not the Bible) —spontaneity. The Holy Spirit can work through our preparation before the church gathers just as effectively as He can work in our gatherings. I'm not suggesting that people praying publicly necessarily have to write their prayers and then read them. But leaders do serve their congregations by spending an hour ahead of time looking through the Scriptures and considering how to pray according to God's priorities and patterns, and perhaps jotting down a few notes.

As individuals and as churches, we should do all we can to align our prayers to the priorities and patterns of the Bible. To that end, I believe we do well, when possible, to mimic the very language of the Bible.

Corporate Prayer— Building Others Up

There is one last principle worth observing as we're thinking about the reverberations of the Word in the prayers of the corporate assembly. This principle comes from Paul: "Let all things be done for building up" (1 Cor. 14:26; also, vv. 4–5, 12, 17–19, 31, 40). Principally, this means that a person praying publicly is addressing both God *and* the congregation. Yes,

God is the primary audience, but there is a secondary audience. Generally speaking, someone leading in public prayer

- should pray "We" not "I," as in "Our Father…";
- should help the congregation to take ownership of one another—one another's praises and laments—remembering when "one member suffers, all suffer"; when "one member is honored, all rejoice" (1 Cor. 12:26); and
- is teaching the congregation to pray by setting the example of biblical prayer—its purposes, priorities, and patterns. Church leaders should shepherd their churches from being concerned only about their own physical welfare to also being interested in their own spiritual welfare, to also being interested in the physical and spiritual welfare of others, to also being interested in the good of their non-Christian neighbors, to also being interested in the good of other churches locally and internationally. D. A. Carson has written that two sources have largely shaped his own prayer life: the Scriptures and more mature Christians.

In summary, aim to unite the church around this growing ambition: "Hallowed be your name, your kingdom come, your will be done, on earth as it is in heaven."

The Measure of a Church

To adapt J. I. Packer's words, we might say that prayer is the measure of a church, spiritually, in a way that nothing else is. When a ninety-minute Sunday service includes less than five minutes of prayer, you can see whom they really trust. When the majority of a church's prayer lists consists of health requests, you can see what the church really values. When a church does not take time to deliberately praise God for who He is, apart from anything He's done for us, you get an idea of how big and majestic their God is, or isn't.

Alternatively, a church being formed by God's Word can't help but echo God's words in its prayer. My own recommendation is that our church gatherings should devote exclusive time to praising God in prayer. Then more time to confessing sin. Then more time to thanking God. And then more time to interceding for the church, for other churches, for the neighborhood and city, for all kinds of authorities, for Christians and churches around the world. In a ninety-minute service, for example, why not include four sessions of praying from five to ten minutes each?

Much of a church's prayer list should look strange and even useless to non-Christians.

Furthermore, God's Word should reverberate in the private prayers of the saints. The points of Sunday's sermon should be heard in prayers around the family dinner table, between two accountability partners, and at the bedside. More and more faces and names in the church directory should also be making their appearance in those private prayers.

In my church, we encourage people to pray straight through the membership directory. How do you pray for people you don't know? Pray Bible.

Some things on a church's prayer list should make sense to non-Christians, as with prayer for acute health situations, or prayer for the good of our neighborhood and city.

But much of a church's prayer list should look strange and even useless to non-Christians: "Please pray that . . . our children would trust in the gospel; we would be faithful in preaching and in listening to God's Word; the church down the street would prosper; a church on the other side of the planet would prosper; God would make us sacrificial with our money and time; we would grow in a culture of transparency in one another's lives; we would be united in spite of cultural, economic, and generational differences; our members would be faithful in evangelism."

That's the sort of stuff a non-Christian might hear and say, "What? Who cares!" Yet that is the glorious picture of a praying church—God's people wanting what God wants. When you witness praying like this, you can be sure that someone else's prayers are being answered in the very thing you're looking at.

Note

1. J. I. Packer, *My Path of Prayer*, David Hanes, ed. (Worthing, West Sussex: Henry E. Walter, 1982), 56.; as cited in D. A. Carson, *A Call to Spiritual Reformation* (Grand Rapids: Baker, 1992), 17.

Recommended Reading

Carson, D. A. *Call to Spiritual Reformation: Priorities from Paul and His Prayers.* Downers Grove, Ill.: InterVarsity, 1992.

Miller, Paul. *A Praying Life.* Colorado Springs: NavPress, 2009.

Sproul, R. C. *The Prayer of the Lord.* Lake Mary, Fla.: Reformation Trust, 2009.

10 } the reverberation disciples

Relationships in the church can be hard, can't they? They can be sticky. They can involve you in complicated situations. And often the fruit of your ministry doesn't show for a long time.

Just consider what kind of conversations come up between two friends who care for each other spiritually:

"How's your relationship with God?"

"Brother, Christians shouldn't do that."

"I struggle with that sin as well."

"I'm not sure what God is doing."

"You must repent."

"Yes, that is a tough passage."

"I am so sorry you are going through this."

"It happened again?!"

"Wait for God's timing."

In contrast, events and programs feel crisp and clean. Yes, lots of hard work is involved in planning an event. You make some calls, you print some flyers, you work a few late nights. But then people come, people have a good time, people pat you on the back, and that's that.

Compared to relationships, events and programs make me think of ice skates gliding across ice. Relationships make me think of gum on the bottom of a shoe on a hot day.

That's probably why it's so easy to default toward thinking of the local church's work in terms of programs and events. They're easy to measure, and they produce visible results.

Of course, we all know where Jesus did His ministry—as well as Paul and the rest of the apostles. They did their work in the context of relationships. Lots of people. Lots of problems. Lots of stickiness. With delayed results.

We've been following the reverberations of God's Word through different areas of the church's life—from the evangelist, to the individual's heart, to the sermon, to the music, to the praying. But relationships are where the story culminates.

The Bible comes in and bounces around between church members. It reverberates in the life of the community. Things will get sticky, but little by little, the reprogramming work of the Word changes the nature of the relationships within a church, bringing love and unity. Members begin to want better, holier things for one another. They begin to speak to one another differently, and to serve one another more. They help each other fight sin.

Sometimes God's Word creates relationships where none existed. Sometimes it transforms and reorients relationships that already existed. But all these relationships begin *to follow* the Word together. This is the heart of discipleship—helping other people follow the Word.

In this chapter, we'll consider the reverberating Word's work in church membership, then in discipleship, and finally in two subcategories of discipleship: counseling and discipline.

Church Membership

Earlier I said, "The Bible comes in and bounces around between church members." Why did I say "church members" and not just "Christians"?

I could have. The Word *should* bounce around between all Christians. Yet I said church members because the ordinary Christian life, at least in the Bible, is lived primarily in unity with a local church. Through baptism and the Lord's Supper, the local church publicly recognizes our professions of faith in the Word, just like Jesus affirmed Peter's profession of faith when Peter recognized Jesus as "the Christ" (Matt. 16:16). Jesus tells Peter that He would establish His church upon Peter and people like him who rightly confess that Jesus is the Christ (vv. 17–19).

The first function of church membership, then, is to publicly affirm our professions of faith in the Word of the gospel. We become Christians by confessing with our mouths "Jesus is Lord" or "the Christ," understanding that His lordship was established through His propitiating death and victorious resurrection (e.g., John 20:31; Acts 17:3; Rom. 10:9; 1 Cor. 12:3, etc.). But Christ has given the church on earth—the local church—authority to publicly validate our profession before the world, almost like the White House press secretary is specifically authorized to say, "Yes, the president said that" or "No, he did not." This is what the local church does through baptism and the Lord's Supper.

The second function of church membership is to exercise oversight of our discipleship to Christ while we're on earth. As church members, we affirm and exercise oversight of the discipleship for one another, like a salvation co-op. We do this to spur one another to love and good deeds, and we do this in case someone's profession of faith in the Word ceases to be credible. The latter scenario leads to church discipline, which I discuss below.

In other words, Jesus doesn't adopt us into His family at conversion and then leave us to raise ourselves. No, He places us in local assemblies that teach and take care of us as Christians. Or here's another analogy. A team owner hires and pays the players. That's Jesus. But the team owner tells the players to report to the coach, who runs the drills and call the plays. That's the local church. Church membership, then, is our submission to this coach—to the affirmation and oversight of the whole assembly.[1]

A third function of church membership is to establish a people among whom Jesus can place ministers of the Word. Jesus clearly means to give gifts of pastors and teachers to *someone* (Eph. 4:11). And He means for *someone* to submit to their instruction and example (Heb. 13:7, 17). Who is that someone? It's the membership of a local church. There is a special blessing attached to those who have been gifted to teach God's Word. And the membership of a local church helps to create the opportunity for this blessing by submitting to their pastors and even by paying for them (1 Cor. 9:11–14; also Matt. 10:10; Gal. 6:6; 1 Tim. 5:17–18).

So in the ordinary course of the Christian life, the Word comes in and bounces around among church members, those who have publicly and formally identified themselves with the Word who was made flesh.

Beyond partaking in baptism and the Lord's Supper, what does church membership look like in action? That brings us to discipleship.

Discipleship

The other night my wife placed cut-up strawberries on the tray of my one-year-old daughter's high chair, and said, "Here you go, Madeline: strawberries!" A second later, my four-year-old daughter parroted her mother's words and voice inflection exactly: "Here you go, Madeline: strawberries!" She even pretended to place strawberries on the high-chair tray.

Why did my four-year-old do that? Because she was created by God as an imaging creature. She's built to image something. So she mimics all sorts of things around her, from the tone of her mother's voice, to the mannerisms of her friends, to the twirling of the princesses in her favorite movies. Most of all, she images what she loves. Wonderfully, she loves her mommy, and so increasingly acts like her.

My daughter, of course, is built like every son and daughter of Adam. All of us are imaging machines. We learn by copying, we copy what we love, and then we become like those things and project them. That's why friends and communities of people act like one another. They love the affirmation they receive from being included in the group. So they begin listening to the same music, wearing the same clothes, mimicking one another's speech patterns, adopting similar sets of moral standards, and more. Welcome to the nature of human culture.

Beginning with the fall, we began imaging one another instead of God.

God designed us this way. The bad news is that, beginning with the fall, we began imaging one another instead of God. The good news is that, with the coming of God's Son, we can now behold a man who is the perfect image of God (Col. 1:15; Heb. 1:3). Like Father, like Son.

What's more, the church is being conformed to the image of the Son (Rom. 8:29; 1 Cor. 15:49, 2 Cor. 3:18). Like Father, like Son, and like sons.

Building on this foundation, let me make three initial statements about discipleship in a church.

First, discipleship works through affection, instruction, and imitation. Paul shows us what discipleship looks like when he writes, "Be imitators of me, as I am of Christ" (1 Cor. 11:1; see also 1 Cor. 4:16; Eph. 5:1; Phil. 3:17; 1 Thess. 1:6; 2:14; 2 Thess. 3:7, 9; Heb. 6:12; 13:7; 3 John 11). He has been instructing the church at Corinth for ten chapters, and then he points to his own example.

We, too, want to listen to those who teach us God's Word, and then we want to imitate their lives. We do all of this, of course, because Christ and His people have become uppermost in our affections.

Affection. Instruction. Imitation.

In my life, this began with my father. My dad taught and modeled God's fatherly compassion and forgiveness for me. As I grew older, other men shared the work of teaching me what Christ is like. Jeff taught and modeled Christ's love for the lost. Mark described and pictured the Son's devotion to the Father's words. Dan demonstrated Christ's patience; Chip, His tender care. I could keep going: Tom, Bruce, Shawn, Steve, Eric, Matt, Thabiti, Michael, and still more—all of them teaching and modeling something about Jesus for me.

These are my disciplers. I have loved them, and so my heart has been drawn to imitating their lives and doctrine. I desire their company. I trust them, and attempt, at every opportunity, to humble myself before their words and their example. I invite their instruction and rebuke.

In turn, I attempt to open up my life to younger brothers

in the faith. Discipling younger brothers means letting them watch my marriage, my parenting, my eldering, my evangelism, and my fight against sin, all the while talking to them about why I do what I do.

Second, discipleship affirms differences. Though discipleship works through following or imitating, it also works through discovering and affirming one another's differences, particularly in the context of the local church and the different gifts we have received.

Paul writes, "If the whole body were an eye, where would be the sense of hearing? If the whole body were an ear, where would be the sense of smell? But as it is, God arranged the members in the body, each one of them, as he chose" (1 Cor. 12:17–18).

Peter, likewise, writes, "As each has received a gift, use it to serve one another, as good stewards of God's varied grace" (1 Peter 4:10).

The call of discipleship is the call to follow and imitate. This is not a call that smothers differences. Instead, it highlights Holy Spirit-assigned distinctives, and calls everyone to use those distinct characteristics and gifts to the same end— serving the one body of Christ.

I'm not exactly like any of the men I named above. The beauty of the church is that I can learn a little more about Jesus from each individual, and so benefit from everyone in learning to exercise whatever gifts the Spirit has given me. This brings us to a third point.

Third, discipleship is church-wide. Those Christians who keep themselves at arm's length from the local church are impoverished. They deprive themselves of the opportunity to learn more about the one they claim to love, Jesus, in the different faces of their fellow members, old and young, salty and sweet.

Indulge me one more moment to look around the room at my own church. There's Li. She makes me think of Christ's quiet humble service. And there's Scott, who's utterly careful that Christ's sheep don't fall into sin. Over there are Bob and Maxine, who teach me about our Savior's perseverance. You get the point. Discipleship doesn't only work between the older man and the younger man, and the older woman and the younger woman, though that might be primary. Every member of the body needs the whole body. "The eye cannot say to the hand, 'I have no need of you,' nor again the head to the feet, 'I have no need of you'" (1 Cor. 12:21).

Through all of this, the Word leads and the church follows, as we help one another to follow Jesus Christ:

> *Therefore each of you must put off falsehood and speak truthfully to his neighbor, for we are all members of one body.* (Eph. 4:25 NIV)

> *Do not let any unwholesome talk come out of your mouths, but only what is helpful for building others up according to their needs, that it may benefit those who listen.* (Eph. 4:29 NIV)

> *But exhort one another every day, as long as it is called "today," that none of you may be hardened by the deceitfulness of sin.* (Heb. 3:13)

Counseling: Discipleship in the Tougher Cases

I don't know of any reason, from a biblical perspective, to distinguish counseling from discipleship. They are the same thing: helping other brothers and sisters in the church to follow Christ by embracing the Word of His gospel.

The difference lies in the concentrated and (typically) issue-specific nature of counseling. The nature and depth of a particular sin or struggle call for more intensive treatment. In that sense, counseling is a subcategory of discipleship. We might call it "discipleship in the tougher cases." It makes me think of passages like the following:

> *Have mercy on those who doubt; save others by snatching them out of the fire; to others show mercy with fear, hating even the garment stained by the flesh.* (Jude 22–23)

> *Brothers, if anyone is caught in any transgression, you who are spiritual should restore him in a spirit of gentleness.* (Gal. 6:1)

Both Jude and Paul seem to be referring to struggles that require extra attention.

That's not to say they require attention outside the local church. I believe that counseling, like discipleship, should primarily occur within the context of the local church. Several reasons commend this. *First, placing counseling in a church means placing it under the elders or pastors* who have been charged with "keeping watch of your souls" and who "will have to give an account" (Heb. 13:17). An outside counselor has not been given this charge. Plus, a pastor's love for the counselee should far exceed what an outsider will offer. Now, there may be times when a pastor feels ill-equipped and wisely decides to involve outsiders, particularly when psychiatric issues are involved. But he should remain involved in the process. That's his job.

Of course, most churches have more counseling needs than the elders can fulfill. Yet this brings us to the *second advantage of church-based counseling: It requires the leaders "to equip the saints for the work of ministry"* by training their members for *"speaking the truth in love"* to one another (Eph. 4:12, 15). It requires them to train their people to counsel one another. This, in turn, will grow the whole church in the unity of faith, maturity, love, and fullness of Christ (vv. 13–16). My underlying assumption here, of course, is that the most useful tool in counseling is the gospel and the Word of God. And this tool is in the possession of every church member. No graduate degrees required.

Remember, discipleship works by affection, instruction, and imitation.

Third, church-based counseling means that the counselor and the counselee sit under the same ministry of the Word, sing the same songs, participate in the same ministries, and walk among the same friends and families. This gives the counselor multiple windows into the counselee's life. He's not limited to what the counselee says during an appointment. He knows what the counselee is being taught. And he can draw in other members of the body to assist ("How would you feel about having lunch with Jim? He's happy to talk about what God has taught him in this area."). Remember, discipleship works by affection, instruction, and imitation. Outside referrals can have their use, but the sequestered and anonymous forty-five minute appointment with an outsider mostly removes affection and imitation from the equation.

Placing the ministry of counseling back into the local church requires church leaders (1) to cultivate a culture of discipleship where members build into one another's lives, and (2) to train their members to care for one another in the tougher cases.

Discipline:
Discipleship in the Toughest Cases

Discipleship includes correcting sin. In fact disciplining sin has a prominent part of discipleship; notice that the words "discipleship" and "discipline" have the same etymological root. The math teacher does not just say to the student, "Here, imitate what I do." He also corrects the student's mistakes. So it goes for the Christian life in the church.

Church discipline is the process of correcting sin in the church body. In most occasions, it begins when one member privately confronts another. If the sinner repents, the discipline stops. If he doesn't, the member will involve two or three others in order to assess the situation and determine if there's a real problem. If they agree there is a problem, and the sinner still doesn't repent, they will bring it to the whole church. And if the sinner does not respond to the church, he will be ex*communion*ed: excluded from the Lord's Table and church membership (see Jesus' instructions in Matt. 18:15–17). This is what we might call discipleship in the toughest cases. We remove a person, Paul says, so that he or she might repent of sin, and be saved on the day of the Lord (1 Cor. 5:5).

Out of discipline, wonderfully, comes life, growth, and health.

Removing a person from church membership is what a church must do when the reverberating of God's Word appears to have grown utterly silent in someone's heart. Given a choice between obedience to God's Word and a particular sin, the individual chooses the sin. And he shows no sign of wanting to do otherwise. It's not any sin, of course. It's an unrepentant sin. It's a serious sin. And it's a sin that can be seen with the eyes or heard with the ears. The Lord has not given us the ability to judge the heart, so a church should not discipline for suspected sins of the heart, like pride or greed. We can only assess by external fruit (Matt. 3:8; 7:17–20). But based on that external fruit, discipline must happen when a person's profession of faith in God's gospel Word no longer appears credible.

God calls us to pursue one another in our sin, because that is how God shows His love for us: "The Lord disciplines those he loves, and he punishes everyone he accepts as a son" (Heb. 12:6 NIV). Churches should practice discipline, in other words, for love's sake: love for *the sinner*, love for *weaker sheep* who can be led astray, love for *non-Christian neighbors* who need to see a holy Christian witness, and love for *Christ and His reputation*.

Out of discipline, wonderfully, comes life, growth, and health: "God disciplines us for our good, that we may share in his holiness. No discipline seems pleasant at the time, but painful. Later on, however, it produces a harvest of righteousness and peace for those who have been trained by it" (Heb. 12:10–11 NIV). The phrase "a harvest of righteousness and peace" makes me think of rolling fields of golden wheat. Only we're talking about golden fields of righteousness and peace. Isn't that a beautiful picture?

The Word Lived Out by Believers

D. A. Carson, we read in the last chapter, attributed growth in his prayer life to Scripture and the example of more mature Christians. I think we can say the same thing about life within the church generally: We grow as Christ's disciples as we *hear* Christ's Word, and as we *see* it lived out by mature believers. The Word points the way to maturity. The mature believer pictures it.

Paul once said to Timothy, "You, however, have followed my teaching, my conduct, my aim in life, my faith, my patience,

my love, my steadfastness, my persecutions and sufferings" (2 Tim.
3:10–11). I hope there are men on this earth who could say the
same thing to me. And that should be true of every Christian.
At the same time, it's not just one or two individuals to
whom we should look. It's the whole church body "speaking
the truth in love, [that we may] in all things grow up into
him who is the Head, that is, Christ. From him the whole
body, joined and held together by every supporting ligament,
grows and builds itself up in love, as each part does its work"
(Eph. 4:15–16 NIV).

Note

1. For a biblical and theological argument for the local church's represen-
tative authority and our individual obligation to submit to the church, see
chapter 4 of Jonathan Leeman, *The Church and the Surprising Offense of
God's Love* (Wheaton, Ill.: Crossway, 2010).

Recommended Reading

Anyabwile, Thabiti. *What Is a Healthy Church Member?*
Wheaton, Ill.: Crossway, 2008.

Coleman, Robert. *Master Plan of Evangelism.* Grand Rapids:
Revell/Baker, 1998. First published in 1963.

Lane, Timothy S. and Paul David Tripp. *How People Change.*
Greensboro, N.C.: New Growth Press, 2006.

Marshall, Colin and Tony Payne, *Trellis and the Vine.* Kingsford,
Australia: Matthias Media, 2009.

Powlison, David. *Seeing with New Eyes: Counseling and the
Human Condition through the Lens of Scripture.* Phillipsburg, N.J.: P&R, 2003.

_____. *Speaking Truth in Love.* Winston-Salem, N.C.: Punch
Press, 2005.

The "Mini Books" series at www.ccef.org (stores.newgrowthpress.
com/StoreFront.bok).

the reverberation scatters and, once again, invites

11 }

It's common these days to say the church exists for the sake of mission. A number of church leaders have written things like

God → has a church → for His mission → to creation (human and nonhuman).

There's a temporary sense in which this is true. But we need to be careful about the *end* of such statements. The far grander, more ultimate truth swings around like a boomerang and heads back in the opposite direction:

Creation → exists for the church → which exists for the praise
of God's name.

Ultimately, all creation, human and nonhuman, exists for
the sake of the church, not the other way around (see 1 Cor.
3:21–23). And the church exists for the sake of God. Does this
sound shocking? It is. Creation eagerly waits for the sons of God
to be revealed, Paul says. And it groans to be released from its
present decay so that it might enjoy a freedom befitting them
(see Rom. 8:19–21).

God's Ultimate Plan

One day, we will no longer conform ourselves to creation,
but creation will conform itself to us. What comfort that is for
the hurting! I heard John Piper speak of encouraging the parents of a handicapped child, "Right now, this child's body has
been caught in the curse of creation. But one day creation will
conform itself to Him and be His servant."

As for human creation, Paul says that God will judge the
ungodly "in order to make known the riches of his glory for vessels of mercy" (Rom. 9:23). God will judge the unrepentant,
in other words, so that the repentant will marvel at God's
mercy to them. I don't understand how this could be, but this
is what the Bible says. It must be true, and it must be good.
Keep in mind, the church is not the *end* of creation either.
Paul also says that the church exists so that God may hold it
up as a trophy of His "manifold wisdom" (Eph. 3:10). It exists,
not finally for the world, but for God's praise (e.g., Isa. 48:8–
11; Ezek. 36:22ff.; Rom. 11:36).

So does God have a church for His mission to the world?
Yes, but it's to tell the world to join the church. That's where
the real action of praise and glory and joy happen. To put it
another way, the gathered church must scatter, but it scatters

to gather others in. It's like a boomerang: we go out to bring back. To shout, "Come to the wedding feast!" (Isa. 25; 55; Matt. 22:1ff.)

Our Mission to the World

Don't miss what this means. There is something supremely special about the gathered church—so special that Jesus tells His followers that the world will know we are His disciples *by our love for one another* (see John 13:34–35). So special that Paul tells us, "Do good to everyone, and *especially to those who are of the household of faith*" (Gal. 6:10, italics added). Christians should love all people, but they should have a special love for the gathered church, even as a man should love all women, but have a special love for his wife.

Does that mean the church can forget about the world? Just the opposite. If a church truly loves God and the fame of *His* name, it is jealous for more and more people to know and praise Him. Every conversion means one more mouth is praising God, and every church planted is a chorus of mouths. Our love for the world is born out of our love for God. The greater our love for God, the greater our desire for others to display God's glory by enjoying Him. We know how good and sweet He is.

Walking through my neighborhood the other day, I imagined what it would be like if literally everyone in my little Washington suburb of six thousand people knew and loved God. Can you picture it? What rejoicing and celebration! What love and peace! Slowly, my heart is learning to love God. And the more it really does, the more it loves my six thousand neighbors. I want them to know Him.

The Father sent the Son to gather worshipers of God, and He sends us to do the same (John 20:21). So we go, like Him, in love.

How do we love the world best? I believe a Christian should love the world, in some respects, like I love my children. I love my children by providing for their physical, social, and emotional needs. I cannot imagine *not* loving them in these ways. Yet I love them most of all—I love them best— by raising them "in the discipline and instruction of the Lord" (Eph. 6:4). All my love for them converges at this central point—pointing them to the words of a book that testifies of Him who is the source of all love. My greatest hope for them is that they would know the love of my Savior, even if it would cost them their lives, lives which I hold so very precious. It's only the truth of God's Word that can give them true freedom and true life.

God's Word must reverberate out the church building doors and into the world.

So churches scatter to love their neighbors, doing good to others physically and socially. Yet all their love should converge in this central and most important place—inviting the world to accept God's promise of forgiveness through Christ and to join the church in enjoying and praising this forgiving God.

God's Word must reverberate out the church building doors and into the world.

Our Message to the World

The news that we speak is, in one sense, the news of the whole Bible. But that news can be summarized in the headline-succinct words of the gospel. What is the gospel? It's the good news that the Son of God has come to save a people for Himself and establish His life-giving, eternal rule in their lives through His own death and resurrection. Here's the message in four parts:

- God, who is perfectly holy, just, and good, created us to display His glorious character and rule.
- We rebelled, choosing to display our own glory and follow our own rule, earning God's just wrath against such sin.
- God sent His Son to reestablish God's rule by living the perfect God-imaging life, dying on the cross to pay the penalty for God's wrath against sin, and rising in victory over sin and death.
- We are now called to repent of our sinful self-rule, confess Jesus as Lord, put our trust wholly in His finished work on the cross, and live the obedient and free life He means for us to live.

This is the message the church gathers to embrace and celebrate. This is the message it scatters to proclaim and demonstrate.

Our Method

How do we present this gospel?

Pastor Tim Keller, in his study guide *Gospel in Life*, presents five characteristics of how we should share God's good news:

1. *In love:* We share the gospel in love.
2. *Without fear:* We share freed from fear because we no longer need the world's approval. We have God's.
3. *Humbly:* We share not because we have wisdom or righteousness, but because we lack it, and want to point others to the true source.

4. *With hope:* We share knowing that God can save anyone. He saved Saul of Tarsus. He saved us!

5. *Courteously and carefully:* Since we know that God's gracious Word alone saves, we can share it without pushiness or manipulation, and then trust Him with the results.

As we lovingly present this gospel, we must also stress the importance of the decision every person must make. In his book *What Is a Healthy Church,* Pastor Mark Dever says that he attempts to convey three things about the decision to be made:

- The decision is costly, so people must be told to consider it carefully (see Luke 9:62).
- The decision is urgent, so people must be told to make it soon (see Luke 12:20).
- The decision is worth it, so people must be told they won't regret it (see John 10:10).

Serve Your Church and Read Your Bible

The evangelist declares God's Word. And then that Word reverberates outward.

It reverberates in the individual's heart and mind. It reverberates among God's people, gathering the church. It reverberates through the sermon. It reverberates through song. It reverberates through prayer. It reverberates in relationships. And it reverberates outward once more as the church scatters, each man and woman equipped as an evangelist.

That's been the story of this book. God gives life through His Spirit and Word.

What does that mean for you? First, it means joining a church that gathers for the Word, or helping your church become that kind of church.

Second, it means making sure the reverberating of God's Word does not stop at noon on Sunday but continues all week long. So put this book down and go read the Bible. Then find someone—a Christian or a non-Christian—and tell him or her what you read.

Here, I'll start. Just this morning, I read 2 Timothy in my quiet time. And these two verses struck me:

Follow the pattern of the sound words that you have heard from me, in the faith and love that are in Christ Jesus. By the Holy Spirit who dwells within us, guard the good deposit entrusted to you. (2 Tim. 1:13–14)

What do you think that means?

Why We Love The Church

Christianity Today Book of the Year Winner in 2010

Church/Pastoral Leadership Category

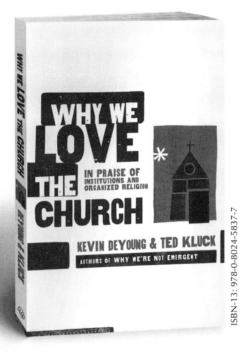

ISBN-13: 978-0-8024-5837-7

Authors Kevin DeYoung and Ted Kluck present the case for loving the local church. Their newest book paints a picture of the local church in all its biblical and real life guts, gaffes, and glory in an effort to edify local congregations and entice the disaffected back to the fold. It provides a solid biblical mandate to love and be part of the body of Christ and counteract the "leave church" books that trumpet rebellion and individual felt needs.

Find out more, read a sample chapter, and even download a free study guide at **WeLoveTheChurch.com**